Herbert Fiessinger

Reichenau Abbey

and the Great Power Venice

Forged Imperial Charters and Intrigues

Front cover: Mittelzell Minster, picture postcard from 1920, painted by Vinzenz Marschall (1889-1959)

The rich Venetian places his right hand on the shrine and with his left hand pulls a stone out of a kettle of boiling water without scalding himself. With this miracle, he testifies to the authenticity of the relic.
Scene at the shrine of St Mark the Evangelist, Reichenau-Mittelzell. Around 1303.

Herbert Fiessinger

Reichenau Abbey

and the

Great Power Venice

Forged Imperial Charters and Intrigues

Herbert Fiessinger:
Reichenau Abbey
and the Great Power Venice
Forged Imperial Charters and Intrigues

Origin:
"Kloster Reichenau im Zeichen des Geflügelten Löwen",
2023.
"Das Kloster Reichenau und die Großmacht Venedig", 2025.

Copyright 2025 Herbert Fießinger

ISBN: **978-3-8192-3020-2**

Die Deutsche Nationalbibliothek verzeichnet diese Publikation
in der Deutschen Nationalbibliografie; detaillierte
bibliografische Daten sind im Internet über dnb.dnb.de
abrufbar.

Publish: BoD · Books on Demand GmbH, Überseering 33,
22297 Hamburg, bod@bod.de
Print: Libri Plureos GmbH, Friedensallee 273, 22763 Hamburg

Content

Description

The Reichenau monastery in Lake Constance / southern Germany experienced rapid growth in the Middle Ages and became immeasurably rich through illumination of church books and through the property of their noble monks. The patron saint of the monastery was St. Mark the Evangelist. Reichenau claimed that the relic of St. Mark was bought from the Doge of Venice in 830. With this, the monastery got in conflict with the Republic of Venice, which also claimed that the bones of this saint lie in St. Mark's Basilica in Venice. - Venice, before 1094, chose the Winged Lion as the symbol of their republic, the Babylonian symbol of absolute power. Because of the rivalry between Venice and Reichenau, the Serenissima Venice subsequently did everything possible to damage the Reichenau abbey. As a result, the conditions in the monastery quickly became unbearable, and the monks' morale completely went down. The monastery became impoverished as a result and experienced an unprecedented rapid decline from around the year 1100. To the disadvantage of the Reichenau monastery, Venice forged documents (imperial charters), which is to be shown by several documents from the village of Göggingen. -

The Reichenau Monastery was allegedly built in 724 by Bishop Pirmin and will be celebrating its 1300th anniversary in 2024. By uncovering various miracle stories as an invention, it can be shown that Reichenau, on the other hand, was first founded not before the beginning of the 10th century. By this Pirmin and many other people are inventions of the Middle Ages. The early history of the Reichenau monastery is different from what is taught. These new findings thus also support the thesis of Dr. Heribert Illig on his "invented Middle Ages 614-911".

Foreword

"St Mark, we salute you". It is Corpus Christi Day in the year 2023 and the rather modestly sized procession is coming down the street in bright sunshine. Standing at the side of the road, the historical town defence force, dressed in white, yellow and red, stands at attention with rifles and trumpets and provides musical accompaniment for the faithful. Festively dressed men carry small and medium-sized golden shrines with holy relics and turn off to the right to the forecourt of Reichenau Cathedral, where a small, rather unadorned altar and a short flower path have been erected, and where local women in their traditional costumes with their black bonnets on their heads are already waiting. The bearers of the holy shrines are followed by splendidly dressed women, and as they turn off towards the church square they sing: "Saint Mark, we salute you."

The bones of St Mark the Evangelist have been on the Reichenau since ancient times, and this evangelist was later made the patron saint of the Reichenau-Mittelzell abbey church. Shortly after the year 1300, the golden shrine of St Mark was erected, a copy of which can be admired today with its beautiful relief images at the entrance to the cathedral, and which contains the so-called Heiltum, the relic of St Mark that brings salvation.

The fact that there is something special about this relic, that the unprecedented decline of Reichenau Monastery in the Middle Ages was also caused by these very bones of St Mark, and that St Mark did not always bring salvation to the monastery, will be told here.

> King's Au indeed, rich you once were,
> Oh now, as you are, you have lost almost everything.[1]

July 2023 Herbert Fießinger

---

1   Complaint by Abbot Konrad von Zimmern 1254

Introduction

The location on the island of Reichenau in Lake Constance is unique for the establishment of a monastery. Here, separated from the worldly life of the neighbouring villages by the water, but not too secluded, the spiritual life of a religious order can flourish. The beautiful nature, the water and the view of the distant mountains invite you to quiet contemplation and let you feel the closeness of God. Ora et labora, pray and work. The mild climate favours agricultural work, as well as fishing and viticulture, so a monastery would have had a decent income in the middle ages. The Benedictine monastery in Beuron, not too far away, also lived from their own farming until around 1990. They had a large number of cows in their stables and sold their milk. They had a large garden and sold honey and meat they produced themselves. In 1986, I still remember it well because I was in Beuron a lot that year, the monks were driving around with their tractors and all kinds of machinery.

They were devoted both to life and to God. A healthy mix, it seems to me. And they also ran an arts and crafts business, had a publishing house and a printing press.

So when Reichenau Monastery was founded, one could have imagined a contemplative monastic life there too. However, things turned out quite differently.

Reichenau Monastery experienced a unique period of prosperity around the year 1000, and its glamour has remained to this day.

How often do we still read about the term "monastic glory" in Reichenau? Back then, when the monastery had become rich, the name of the monastery and the island was changed from Au to "die reiche Au" (engl. the rich Au), Reichenau, for good reason. In those days - probably a thousand years ago - it was said that if the abbot of Reichenau wanted to travel to Rome, he could spend the night on his own land every day. The monastery's property stretched from the town Ulm to Italy. And there was also a legend that when the first wagon of the convoy with the feudal dues arrived at Reichenau Abbey from Ulm, the last wagon was still at the city gate in Ulm.

These are undoubtedly literary exaggerations. We come closer to reality when we read:

> ... a monastery that once had around 300 noble vassals and from which four archdukes, 10 counts palatine and margraves, 27 counts and 28 barons and knights held fiefs. A monastery from which 18 archbishops, 60 bishops and 29 abbots emerged for other monasteries. [Güßfeldt p.68, Staiger p.151]

And the many peasant and bourgeois vassals of the many other villages are not even listed above.

Conrad Gröber, the later archbishop, a native of Messkirch, studied the Reichenau in detail. His books are characterised by great expertise. And he also fell under the inexplicable spell of Reichenau when he visited the island around 1922 when he wrote:

> In addition to emperors and kings, cardinals and bishops, artists, art-loving people and industrious researchers, the monastery has also seen many others who would have been better off not coming. But then, while the waves are still rocking us, the melancholy medieval bells ring out, as if we were going to the conventual office over there in silent monastic order. We disembark, but hardly anyone disturbs the atmospheric silence. The island's hard-working country folk, vine-growers and fishermen have always plenty to do on their often remote meadows and fertile fields, in the ascending vineyards and in the swaying barges. It is as if the old monastic solitude surrounds us and the whispering of the mighty trees in the church square whispers mysteriously about the weathered stones of the 10th century. The monks are dead, only their art still speaks from distant times in enigmatic tones, powerful

and full of meaning. [Gröber 1922 p.4]

The inexplicable magic of Reichenau is still omnipresent in me, even though I was able to learn many secrets of the island monastery, both beautiful and not so beautiful. Is it just because my home village of Göggingen was once a Reichenau village? Or does the former cultural flourishing, the inner and outer wealth of the monastery still shine in the collective memory of mankind after a thousand years?

> Hermann the Lame is not exaggerating when he calls Reichenau a monastery ennobled by great men, books and the treasures of its church. [Gröber 1922 p.8]

> We can go even further and say that it was a focal point of Christian life, a meeting place for all scholarship, a spiritual playground for Germanic youth and thus one of the most flourishing centres of culture beyond the Alps. [Gröber 1922 p.9]

And Josef Sauer writes:
'In the scientific and literary fields, Reichenau had an almost universal cultural mission.' [Gröber 1922 p.9]

However, the scientific and literary achievements of the monastery known to us today are few. The cultural mission of which Sauer speaks is much more to be seen in the area of Christian mission, in the world-famous medieval Reichenau book illumination, in the impressive buildings from the Middle Ages, as well as in the universal memory of the former monastic glory, and also in the wealth, nature and flair that the former monastery has been able to preserve to this day. It was not for nothing that it was declared a UNESCO cultural heritage site some years ago.

In the best days of the monastery, when it was still young, Abbot Ermenrich from the cold town of Ellwangen praised Reichenau with such beautiful words:

> Reichenau, flourishing island, how blessed you are above others
> Rich in the treasures of knowledge and the holy spirit of its inhabitants
> Rich in the fruit of the fruit tree and the swelling grapes of the vineyard
> Evermore it blooms on you and the lily is reflected in the lake
> Far thy fame resounds to the misty land of the Britons[2]

And from the same time, when the monastery was not yet in decline, these following uplifting lines must also date from the island:

> Where the waters of the Rhine flow from the Italian Alps
> Into the mighty lake that stretches far to the west,
> There in the midst of the flood rises the lovely island,
> Aue it is called, in the heart of Germania it lies
> Hordes of excellent monks it brought forth.[3]

As late as 1590, when the monastery had long since lost its independence and was subject to the Bishop of Constance, an unknown person wrote of an island monastery that was unrivalled and therefore unique; and he continued: "In the past, it was very fond of wealth ..." and then he wrote: "If you read the chronicle particularly carefully, you will be amazed at how the times have changed, as have the people":

> A beautiful island lies not far away
> in Lake Constance, the old German sea,

---

2   Gröber 1922 Translation by J. Scheffel
3   literally "Augia nomen habens", - The vision of Wetti. The name augia suggests that the Visio Wettini was created in the heyday of the Reichenau around the year 1000, or later

which is well known to many
by us called the Rich-Au.
Pirmin the first abbot
planted the island,
erected a monastery there
years ago, without equal.
In times gone by very inclined to wealth,
as the church treasury still shows,
St Mark's tomb also of that time,
as this book will give an account
what kind of life this monastery led.
If you read the chronicle carefully
you will be astonished
how the times have changed
and in it also the people.[4]
[Brandi II p. XXIV]

Yes, times have changed. After a brief period of prosperity at the highest level, the monastery experienced an incomprehensible and unprecedentedly rapid decline, beginning around the year 1100, which has not yet been understood. Historians see fires around 1250 as the cause, but the abbey was already in steep decline 150 years earlier, and the monastery chronicler Gallus Öheim in the early 16th century writes vaguely of the disagreement between the popes, emperors and princes, which caused the decline of the monastery:

Many people wonder, when they hear of the incredible power of the monastery, how it could have come to such stupidity of decline. The abbots are no less often blamed for having lived so carelessly and dissolutely. There may be some truth in this; I could name several more under whose reign the house of God has declined and not

---

4   adapted to today's language

increased. God knows their names. The truth is that the disunity of the popes and emperors has brought the greatest ruin to the house of God, as well as the disorganisation of the princes, since some wanted to conquer the empire by force, war, robbery and fire.[5] [Brandi II p.23]

So not even Gallus Öheim, the monastery chronicler, can say anything concrete about the cause of the decline.
There were often fires in other monasteries too, and the disunity of the secular lords also affected other monasteries. However, no other monastery experienced such a downfall as Reichenau.

We read things in old written sources that amaze us:

that the Reichenau archivist Odalrich destroyed his own valuable royal charters on his own authority around the year 1150, or scraped off the text and inscribed the royal charters with cheap forgeries instead.

that the foundation charter of the monastery from the year 724 is a forgery.

that apart from very few pieces, no literature was produced on Reichenau, or that it was perhaps destroyed at some point. A book on horticulture, a vision of a monk and a world chronicle from the 11th century, which was largely copied from other sources, that is almost all. So there are only very few writings from the time when Reichenau was still doing well. Nothing of importance came after that, with the exception of the monastery chronicle by Gallus Öheim from the period after 1500, in which much sounds like pure fantasy.

---

5   adapted to today's language

that for a long time the monks were almost without exception aristocratic lords who had never learnt to subordinate themselves and who had nothing else in mind but to eat their way through the monastery and indulge in amusements.

that in 1135 the monks even beat their own abbot, Ludwig von Pfullendorf, to death in his chasuble at Church service in the church in Tuttlingen without being punished.

that the monks openly defied Abbot Burkhard in 1258 when he demanded that they take off their noble vestments and put on the Benedictine habit instead. Two monks then decided to beat their abbot to death over dinner. However, the abbot managed to escape, whereupon the two criminal monks gathered armed followers, plundered the island and chased away all those who remained loyal to the abbot.

that the abbey of Reichenau was at war with the brother monastery of St Gallen (Switzerland) for many years. Both sides hired mercenaries and ravaged each other's lands because of the dishonour of a broken abbot's staff.

It was then that Abbot Diethelm could no longer put up with his own monks, was afraid of them and withdrew completely to his tower in Steckborn.

that Abbot Werner no longer wanted to eat with his own conventuals and instead travelled to Niederzell every day on his little horse and had himself fed there. It is said that the monastery was so poor that it could no longer feed its own abbot.

that only 2 monks lived in the monastery in the early 15th and early 16th centuries.

that the Abbot of Reichenau Brandis probably had the Bishop of Constance murdered in 1356. In any case, the murderers immediately fled to the island and the abbot, who had probably ordered the murder, had them deliciously entertained and rewarded with money.

that a number of Reichenau monks once went to Zurich in the winter of 1368 to take part in knightly tournaments, encountered citizens of Constance on the way and immediately beat each other to death on the street.

that the cellar master and later Abbot Mangold gouged out the eyes of a fisherman from Constance in 1366 because he was catching fish in Reichenau waters.

that the Reichenau abbot intercepted a Constance ship and had nine Constance servants stabbed to death.

that in 1382 the citizens of Constance then destroyed Schopflen Castle in Reichenau and various farms on Reichenau and cut off the heads of nine captured Reichenau servants. - The ruins of Schopflen can still be seen today on Pappelallee-street.

that the monastery in the 14th century had to sell everything that was not nailed down.

that an Abbot Eberhard burnt all the feudal documents.

that an Abbot Werner wanted to sell the bones of St Mark to Venice due to a lack of money, but was forcibly prevented from doing so by the monastery servants.

that the last abbot, Markus, finally betrayed and sold his own monastery in Reichenau and immediately left for Radolfzell with his lavish Judas salary.

that the last monks of the monastery were rebellious in 1757 and had to be driven out of the monastery with 40 soldiers under threat of armed force.

The chroniclers of past centuries reported what seemed interesting to them. They tell us nothing about quiet days and years full of spiritual contemplation and reflection, solemn processions, church festivals and worship, because such things did not seem worth mentioning to them.
One must assume, in order not to see a distorted image, that there must have been such peaceful years. However, even Conrad Gröber, an expert on Reichenau who is not suspected of wanting to denigrate the church, comes to this conclusion:

> After the 11th century and into the 14th century, the embers barely glowed under the piled-up ashes. And if, as was the case under Abbot Diethelm of Krenkingen (1180-1206), it seemed as if a timid crackling and repeated flickering still revealed a remnant of spiritual life, all too soon thereafter came the deadly quiet darkness, even hopeless ruin. In the middle of the 13th century, the abbey no longer even had the strength to appoint an abbot as a result of feuds, lawsuits, senseless waste, poor administration and persistent aristocratic inbreeding. [Gröber 1938 p.12]

> The medieval history of the Au is, to use an image, a sunny, shining, all-promising morning, a dull, even ugly noon and a reasonably beautiful, short evening. [Gröber 1922 p.5]

If you look at the history of Reichenau from a higher perspective, you will notice that the more it celebrated its cult of St Mark, the worse became the state of the Monastery.

And it is also noticeable that the decline of Reichenau coincided with the rise of a great European power: Venice.

What does Reichenau have to do with Venice?
Originally, the two had only one point of contact: both claimed to be in possession of the bones of St Mark the Evangelist.
However, Reichenau subsequently had a number of other connections with Venice that are hardly noticeable at first glance. In order to recognise and understand the true history of Reichenau and its decline, it is therefore necessary to take also a closer look at Venice.
Both Venice and Reichenau invented a variety of miracle stories in connection with their respective church saint Mark, which must be recognised in their entirety for what they are: Fictions and inventions without history. As soon as this is clear, and as soon as the motives behind these inventions are also clear, a completely new early history of Reichenau opens up that has never been told before.

Everything written here is based on the idea that invented stories contain no history.
From this perspective, the forgeries of the Reichenau documents also make sense in a way that has not yet been recognised.
It is perhaps not a good idea to dwell too much on the past, as this can obscure our view of the present. But if the past is denied, the future can be destroyed. The seed of our destiny finds its nourishment in the past.

So what remains?

> Only the three great churches and the marvellous nature, the shimmering lake, the fragrant distances, the sparkling wine and the grateful memory remain of the

old glory - and it is still an unspeakable amount. Everything else is no more. [Gröber 1922 p.11]

Only churches, nature and memory. - Gröber does not mention literary, historical, musical or scientific works. He does not even mention the famous book illumination. Yet the 11th century abbot and singing teacher Bern probably also left us a theory on music and singing. And the song Salve Regina is also often attributed to Hermann the Lame. But it is questionable whether he really wrote it. Nor is it 100% proven whether the illuminations were really created on Reichenau or perhaps in Trier or Echternach.

Apart from the illuminations and the three churches, very little of material significance remains of the former monastery.
A German emperor is said to be buried in Reichenau Minster. If you ask more precisely, you will hear that the grave has been lost. Emperor Karl the Fat (Karl der Dicke), +888, a great benefactor of Reichenau, is his tomb simply allowed to decay, disappear and fall into oblivion?
The same happened to the grave of the generous benefactor Duke Gero (+799), alleged brother-in-law of Charlemagne. His grave has also disappeared.
Like so much of the history of Reichenau, this emperor and this duke are an invention. They and their tomb only existed on paper.
Reichenau was able to salvage much less from the past than other monasteries. Fate has not been kind to Reichenau.

The cathedral in Reichenau-Mittelzell. Engraving from 1840.

The Minster (cathedral). St Mark's tomb on the right

The Early History

Perhaps the earliest mention of Reichenau dates back to Roman times[6], when the Romans conquered the Lake Constance region. A historian of the time reports of an island in Lake Constance that served as a place of retreat for the army, although it is unclear whether he was referring to Reichenau, the island of Lindau or perhaps Mainau. However, Reichenau seems to have been best suited for this military purpose. The proximity to the pacified area south of the Rhine and also the proximity to the strategic river crossing at Constance make Reichenau appear like a forward, temporary military camp. One is also inclined to regard the tower of St. George as the successor to a Roman watchtower, strategically located at the closest point to the mainland.

In any case, this today's tower and the church building of St George are obviously older than the other two churches on Reichenau, both visually and in terms of architectural style. The tower and church of St George must date from a time when the builders were still somewhat inexperienced in building with stone.

Reichenau church St Georg in Oberzell

---

6   in Strabon 16 BC

The Byzantine-looking west apse brings to mind the great patrons of the Reichenau, the Ottonian emperors with their dynastic connection to Byzantium.

Much later, in the Gothic period, when the german master builders had already gained centuries of experience with the construction of stone buildings, they built much lighter and with large windows, much higher and more filigree, with perfect light arches and a supporting stone outer skeleton. We don't see any of this in the Romanesque period and especially not here at St George's. The first building of St George's is therefore probably from the beginning of the Romanesque period (i.e. towards the end of the 10th century) and its current structure is the oldest of the three island churches.

On the other hand, the architectural style of today's cathedral in Mittelzell points to a later construction in the High Middle Ages:

> Friedrich Adler, who first (1869) subjected the church to a serious art-historical examination, describes the side aisle walls and the column at the west entrance of the south aisle as the oldest parts of the building and places them in the time of Wittigowo (986-997). He considers the west choir together with the transept and the outer vestibules to be a remnant of St Mark's Church consecrated after Hermann the Lame under Abbot Berno in 1048. In his opinion, however, the pillar arcades of the central nave belong to a new building begun in 1172 under Diethelm of Krenkingen (1169-1206) (only attested by Bruschius), which is supported by the ornamentation of the capitals (zigzag bar). [Gröber 1922 p.22]

> The current structure of the cathedral is therefore likely to date largely from the middle of the 11th century, built by Abbot Bern, or parts of it built by the building-minded Abbot Wittigo shortly before the year 1000, as the

Romanesque architectural style does not allow an earlier dating, while a later construction in the 12th century can actually be ruled out due to the spiritual and financial hardship. [Gröber 1922 p.71]

Nevertheless, at least the pillar arcades mentioned do not appear to have been built until the end of the Romanesque period, i.e. probably in the time of Diethelm of Krenkingen around 1180, when the monastery had long been in a state of decay.

The church in Niederzell is the youngest of the three Reichenau churches and its current structure dates from after 1080:

After two fires, the foundation building of Niederzell was demolished around 1080 and the current transeptless columned basilica was built on the old foundations, retaining the original dimensions[7]

The foundation building, which was only around 100 years old, was therefore demolished due to a fire. There seem to have been many fires in the past, to which, strangely enough, also stone churches fell victim.

The main current building structures of the three churches therefore date from around 970 at the earliest for Oberzell; partly around 990 (Abbot Wittigo), partly shortly before 1048 (Abbot Bern) for Mittelzell, and after 1080 for Niederzell. The first stone church in Mittelzell was probably built around 940.

The name of the island in the early Middle Ages was 'Au', meaning meadow or fertile lowland. The island has certainly been permanently inhabited since the end of antiquity, as the

---

7   Wikipedia (german) St Peter and Paul (Reichenau-Niederzell)

mild climate favoured life and agriculture there. Until today, however, no remains of settlements from the early Middle Ages have been found on the island. But that doesn't mean anything. "In view of the climatically favoured location of the island, this fact [of no settlement] needs to be explained", writes Michael Richter. [Richter p.4]

The romanesque part of the cathedral in Reichenau-Mittelzell

There are a number of later written, invented and fictitious stories and documents about the early days of Reichenau. A study of the history of Reichenau reveals a whole series of forgeries and legends, where it can be difficult to see the wood for the trees. It is often not easy to distinguish the fiction of the invented events, people and dates from reality.
If one does not attribute any historical value to these stories, then the history of the monastery begins in the early 10th century. It is conceivable that the monastery was founded in connection with the nearby bishopric of Constance, or initiated by it, but there are no records of this.
We must therefore assume that the first building and thus the

foundation of the monastery took place around the year 920, or somewhat earlier.

The monastery gave itself the name: Sintleozes-Au, which means the sinless meadow or the 'Sündlos-Au'. Due to various spellings of this name, the following meaning is also conceivable: Sünd-Lass-Au; let ('lass') in the sense of let away, let off, drop, or let go of sins (for money).

The religiously interpretable meaning of this monastery name alone makes it clear that there could not have been a person called Sintlas, of whom later legends tell.

A few decades later, when the monastery had already become very rich before the year 1000, it was clearly embarrassed to bear a name that was associated with sin, presumably because its inhabitants were anything but sinless. Even before the year 1000, the monastery therefore changed its name back to Au or Aue, latinised Augia. The Latin sources write Augia regalis = royal augia, Augia maioris = great augia and Augia dives = rich augia; the island and the monastery were named after the latter in the vernacular: Reichenau, the rich meadows.

But even after the year 1000, the name Sintleozesau can still be found in documents. This is due to the fact that these documents, which are usually forged, pre-date a supposed early period of Reichenau, when the name Sintleozesau was still in common use. If the forgers had used the new name Augia dives in their documents in the 12th century, for example, the forgery would of course have been immediately recognisable to any insider due to the use of the modern name, and the forgery would have been easily uncovered.

All documents must always be evaluated individually: when were they actually written and to what earlier time are they dated or are they supposed to indicate?

Historians see the beginnings of the monastery in the year

724 and refer to the Vita Pirmini, the life story of the first abbot. But Karl Brandi already saw clearly:

> 'It is obvious that all these different versions of the Vita Pirmini are absolutely worthless for the history of Reichenau according to the place and time of their origin.' [Brandi I p.103]

> The Reichenau document archive contains many forgeries from the period before 1200. [Brandi I p.V]

According to Brandi, only a comprehensive examination of these forged documents would enable historians to shed light on the history of Reichenau. And then Brandi's remarkable statement:

> 'Without this work no firm ground can be gained from the foundation of Reichenau to about 1200, a history of Reichenau in this period is impossible.' [Brandi I p.V]

Michael Richter, on the other hand, does not doubt the alleged foundation date of 724, but sees research as being on thin ice - which seems like a contradiction:

> In the absence of a genuine foundation document, the year 724 is cited as the beginning of the monastery in the poem Visio Wettini by Walafried Strabo, written a century later; I have no good reason to doubt this date for the foundation, but would just like to point out how thin ice we are on when it comes to the beginnings of the island monastery of Reichenau. [Richter p.3]

Giving historical significance to fictionalised stories obscures the view of what really happened. Michael Richter also admits that knowledge about the early days of Reichenau is extremely confused:

> 'Research has reached a dead end; the mysteries surrounding the beginnings of the monastery seem

more insoluble than ever.' [Richter p.3]

Richter assumes that it was founded in 724. However, if we relegate this early foundation to the realm of fairy tales and instead date it to the beginning of the 10th century, everything becomes clear.

The Miracle Stories of St Mark

When the monastery was founded in the early 10th century, its founder from Constance endowed it with the relic and bones of a saint named Valens. Just a few years later, the abbot at the time decided that the abbey was worthy of a greater saint and, for whatever reason, he chose St Mark the Evangelist.

A miracle story was immediately composed and named Miracula Sancti Marci, i.e. the miracle story of St Mark. One can still recognise the obvious connection between Reichenau and the Bishop of Constance when Bishop Noting declared in around 930 that St Mark the Evangelist had to be venerated on Reichenau from then on. It is quite possible that the miracle story was a fabrication of the bishop himself. In any case, the bishop upgraded Reichenau through this act, which clearly shows that Constance and Reichenau were not yet enemies at the time, as it would later be the case.

At the same time, two further relics were invented, namely the relic of the Holy Blood and the jug from the Wedding of Kana, both of which are still on the Reichenau today. The texts "De pretioseo sanguine domini nostri" was written for the relic of the Holy Blood and the "Vita Symeonis Achivi" for the jug of Kana. Nothing is easier to forge and invent than a text. At that time, in the early days of writing in the Alemannic region, an incredibly high, almost magical power of truth must have been associated with a script, a parchment. And that is still the case today.

The veneration of relics always goes hand in hand with making their authenticity credible. Now the writers of the Miracula, perhaps the Bishop of Constance, were faced with the problem of how to make the faithful believe that the existing reliquary in Reichenau contained the bones of St Mark and not the bones of Valens, as had been proclaimed for more than 10 years.
And they solved the problem elegantly: first they described in detail in the Miracula the alleged purchase of St Mark's bones from a high-ranking Venetian who, for whatever reason, is said to have sold these bones to the Bishop of Verona named Ratold. This Ratold, a figure who never existed, is said to have brought the relic to Reichenau. The unnamed Venetian is said to have been able to prove the authenticity of the relic through various miracles, an oath, a trial by fire and the so-called cauldron catch, i.e. dipping his hand into a cauldron full of boiling water without being hurted.

Stories that talk about miracles are generally speaking always untrue, and there is always a reason to find out why the author is lying. If an author includes miracle stories in his narrative, what credibility does the rest of his story have?
And according to the Miracula, the unknown Venetian made the relic buyer Ratold promise not to reveal the identity of St Mark, but to pass himself off as St Valens.
According to the Miracula, this all happened in the year 830, exactly 100 years before Bishop Noting proclaimed St Mark the Evangelist as the new monastery saint.
So St Mark supposedly lay unrecognised for a hundred years under the name Valens on Reichenau. To make the matter a little more credible, the vision of a bishop of Constance was invented in 10th century, to whom St Mark himself said in a dream in around 875 that he should take better care of the

bones, because it was not Valens but he himself, i.e. St Mark, who was lying in the reliquary.

This is a practical way of explaining to the believing people why the real identity of the bones was forgotten for decades, and how the monastery then became aware of the correct identity again. And once again we see a Bishop of Constance playing a role. It must be assumed that the story of St Mark was invented together in Reichenau and Constance.

This is how Reichenau came to have its monastery saint St Mark, which must be described as one of the monastery's two birth defects. Because the later great european power of Venice also claimed to possess a complete body, probably a mummy of St Mark.

> For understandable reasons, however, the Reichenau story of St Mark has always received little attention in Venice: Rather, it was regarded by the Venetians - as, incidentally by the German monumentalists in the 19th century - as an evil work of art or, at best, a free invention. [Dennig/Zettler p.22]

Venice certainly regarded the Reichenau story of St Mark as a fabrication. But the story must have attracted a great attention in Venice nonetheless, because the 'Miracula S. Marci' claims that the relic came to Lake Constance from Venice of all places, i.e. that it was stolen and sold off. And to Venice's great annoyance, the mortal remains of the evangelist were in this monastery north of the Alps, at least that is what was claimed. Venice was of course aware that its own history of St Mark was also a fabrication, as it had invented its own story itself.

Even early on, St Mark apparently only led a niche existence in the Reichenau monastery:

> It is striking that from the second half of the 11th to the
> end of the 13th century, virtually no news of the body of
> St Mark on Augia or external evidence of his veneration
> there can be seen. [Bock]

This was still the case later, when Sebastian Bock continues: ... that the evangelist may not have been one of the most popular saints of the Augia at that time [around 1500]. The only detailed description of a cult of relics in Öheim's chronicle does not concern the highly significant patron saint of the monastery, but the founder of the abbey, Pirmin. The monk reports on Pirmin's veneration in detail and with some sympathy.

Incidentally, Dr. Sebastian Bock is of the opinion that the Miracula "was not put into the world with falsifying intentions".
- But what other purpose could the writing of this miracle story have had? Nothing happens without intention. And the intention here was to make the authenticity of St Mark's relic credible. If that is not a falsifying intention!

Around the year 920, Venice was still under Byzantine rule. It then became independent and acquired fabulous wealth through its trade with the Orient, its financial transactions and the slave trade. After the year 1000, Venice can justifiably be described as a major european power. Although Venice's land size always remained very small, this disadvantage was compensated for on the one hand by its huge merchant and war fleet, which was built from 1104 in the Arsenal shipyard using assembly line labour, and on the other hand by its superior diplomacy and inexhaustible financial resources, which allowed Venice to recruit mercenaries in very large numbers if necessary and have them fight for Venice. The ability to grant loans of almost any amount also enabled

Venice to gain great influence in Europe. But also great enmity, as we shall see.

Here in Venice, from the 11th century onwards, people incarnated whose self-image was characterised by absolute power. In their search for a symbol of their universal claim to power, they looked to the East. And they found such a symbol in the Babylonian sign of the zodiac: it was the lion.
In astrology, the zodiac sign of Leo still symbolises kingship, power and dominion today. Even the Babylonian rulers were aware of the importance of the lion for their worldly power. The Babylonian lion can still be admired today in the Pergamon Museum in Berlin and the British Museum in London. The Greek sphinx, the symbol of opacity and mystery, is also shown as a winged lion.

For a long time, the patron saint of Venice was St Theodore. When Venice became a great power after the year 1000 and wanted to demonstrate this understanding of great power to the outside world by building a new cathedral, the Serenissima, the Most Serene Republic of Venice, decided to change its patron saint. The symbol for St Mark the Evangelist had been the lion since the biblical Book of Revelation, and this connection was also derived from the Old Testament, the Book of Ezekiel, at an early stage.
The lion was thus the link between St Mark the Evangelist and the absolute claim to power that Venice wanted to embody. For this reason, Venice decided to adopt St Mark as its new republican saint.
Between the years 1063 and 1094, St Mark's Cathedral was built in Venice, and at the same time[8] the so-called Translatio was invented in Venice, i.e. the story of how the mummy of St

____

8   Nelson McCleary: Note storiche ed archéologiche sul testo della Translatio Sancti Marci 1933; he names the period 1050 to 1094 for the creation of the Translatio

Mark was supposedly transferred from Alexandria to Venice.

The translatio was set in the year 829, strikingly one year before the Reichenau Miracula. Alexandria was under Muslim rule and St Mark lay in the church there with his miraculously uncorrupted body. Two Venetians had travelled to Alexandria, convinced the two church administrators there that St Mark would be better off in Venice because of the insecurity caused by the Muslims, and then loaded the mummy onto their ship, where various miracles took place. Firstly, the mummy in Alexandria gave off an inexplicable odour, and secondly, Mark saved the ship from sinking in a storm during the crossing.

Alfons Zettler cites an unfortunately unexplained anonymous source from Fleury from the 10th century as an indication that the Venetian translation report was already widespread "in the 9th and 10th centuries". [Dennig/Zettler p.32]
According to Zettler, this text indicates that the translatio was recorded "no later than the middle of the 9th century" by a well-informed observer from Venice.

However, invented stories usually have no history. This translation story was not handed down to us by a well-informed observer, but by a good story writer and inventer.
So, in 1094, St Mark the Evangelist became the patron saint of Venice.
Today's historians do not believe in the miracles that are said to have occurred in the Venetian Translatio and the Miracula of Reichenau. However, they usually admit that both stories have a kernel of truth.

Sebastian Bock is one of the few who takes a very critical view of the historicity of the Miracula:
> The Miracula S. Marci can in no way be used as a serious, even rudimentary source for the origin of the

relics of St Mark from Venice, the biography of Ratold of Verona, the foundation of Radolfzell, the research into the older history of Venice or the construction of a basilica dedicated to the cult of St Mark on Reichenau in the late 9th century. The only historically accurate fact regarding the relics of St Mark on Reichenau in the Miracula S. Marci is probably only the approval of the cult of St Mark by Bishop Noting in the period around 930. [Bock]

However, many historians believe that the bones of St Mark were actually stolen from Alexandria in 829 and that these bones were sold to Reichenau a year later.
It makes no sense that the precious relic should have been sold again just one year after its fortunate acquisition. The monastery chronicler Hermann the Lame recognised this gap in credibility around the year 1050 and commented the Reichenau Miracula with another fiction: the unknown Venetian who sold the relic to Ratold was the Doge of Venice himself. - After all, who else but the Doge had the power to sell his own church treasure?
Hermann the Lame's assertion gives the Miracula more credibility, but the Venetians must not have liked the claim that their own doge had proved to be a traitor in 830. Hermann was thus certain to turn the Venetians against the monastery in the period that followed and thus also severely damaged his own credibility: Hermann proved to be a tendentious inventor of stories and not a serious historian.

For some reason, St Mark was difficult to communicate to the people from the very beginning:
What is striking is the complete lack of findings to date for the period from the official authorisation for diocese-wide cultic veneration of the evangelist and his relics by Bishop Noting (around 930) to the insertion of

translocated particles of St Mark, very probably of Reichenau provenance, in the years 1021 and 1052/1065 ...

Remarkably, everything does not point to an immediate success story. There is no reliable evidence for a rapidly flourishing pilgrimage, the inclusion of the saint in the monastic liturgy, an opening up of the sanctuary, the translocation of parts of the bones, the formation of secondary cultural centres, the elevation of the evangelist to official co-patron of the abbey church or any other external radiant effect. [Prof. Sebastian Bock]

Was it just because St Mark was a writing theologian, a non-native from distant Greece, aloof from the common people, or did Reichenau immediately feel the headwind from Venice?

All in all, St Mark seems to have been difficult to communicate as an individual saint. ... Another factor may also have been that the monks on Lake Constance were hardly able to oppose the comprehensive, almost state-political cult that Venice had established around the bones of St Mark in the lagoon city at an early stage [Sebastian Bock]

Around the year 1300, some 200 years after the completion of St Mark's Basilica, the so-called Apparitio was invented in Venice, a story about the allegedly miraculous recovery of the relic of St Mark in a pillar of the predecessor building of St Mark's Basilica in Venice.

In 1300, an explanation was needed as to why nobody in Venice knew anything about the relic of St Mark from the alleged events of the translatio in 829 until the consecration of St Mark's Basilica in 1094 and why there were no records of it. For this very purpose, the apparitio was invented, i.e. the story of the rediscovery of the relic, which had allegedly been hidden in a pillar between 829 and 1094.

On 25 June 1094, a stone suddenly detached from the pillar and the corpus of St Mark's became visible.

Of course, this does not sound too credible. Just before the cathedral was consecrated, the relic of St Mark appeared by chance, as if by magic, when the patron saint of the church had certainly already been determined during the long construction phase of the cathedral. But believers believe many things.

The apparitio could only be invented when all witnesses to the consecration of St Mark's Cathedral had long since died, and that was around 200 years later, in 1300. No one could therefore contradict the apparitio, no one could say that the apparitio was untrue; there were no more witnesses.

The apparitio served to make the translatio more credible. It is also possible that the apparitio was invented as a reaction to the erection[9] of the golden shrine of St Mark in Reichenau, when the cult of St Mark flared up again on Reichenau.

The new shrine of St Mark certainly made waves all the way down to Venice, as it was most likely commissioned by Queen Elisabeth of Austria and probably made in Constance, and is an excellent and skilful piece of work. Venice probably wanted to use the Apparitio to counter the revival of the cult of St Mark in Reichenau after 1300.

Meanwhile, the cult of St Mark in Venice developed into a state cult:

> [...] In the course of Venice's internal formation and expansion, St Mark grew to become the undisputed and radiant patron saint of the town, eventually epitomising it. The lion, originally the mystical symbol of the evangelist, became the omnipresent state symbol of the lagoon republic, so that the history of Venice could be measured against St Mark and succinctly summarised in his symbol. [...] [Zettler p.541]

---

9   not before 1303, see Sebastian Bock

Fig.: Reichenau book illumination, Gero Codex around 969,
St Mark with the winged lion (above).

The Flowering Period

In addition to the old buildings and the Oberzell wall paintings
in St George's, Reichenau is known and famous today above
all for its medieval book illumination.

In the decades before and after the year 1000, around 40 so-
called gospel books were produced on the island, i.e.
magnificently and colourfully painted missals that were sold
throughout the German Empire and were mostly
commissioned work.

This book illumination laid the foundations for the abbey's

later wealth. However, the abbey could certainly not live on one book sold per year.

The abbey's sudden rise to fame attracted a large number of nobles like a magnet, many of whom were probably of a wealthy and settled age where renunciation was no longer so difficult, and these nobles had to cede a very large sum of money or land to the abbey as a kind of entrance fee. And it is still the case today that a monk or nun in a Christian monastery is no longer allowed to have any property after the novitiate, but must transfer all previous property to the monastery.

Franz Xaver Staiger speaks of 1600 monks[10] who once lived in the Reichenau convent. A number that seems incredibly high, because how were 1600 people to be fed and clothed, how were they to celebrate church service together, what were they to be kept busy with? In addition, there must have been a hundred or more servants and maidservants and many dozens of construction workers when building work was underway.

You can only feed 1600 people who do not work for their own living if there is a constant external inflow of money. If this stops, things go downhill quickly.

However, the information provided by archivist Aloys Schulte seems much more realistic. According to him, there were 96 souls in the monastery under Abbot Alawich (934-958): 1 abbot, 30 priests, 23 deacons, 18 subdeacons, 23 monks and one unnamed monk. In 1267, all the brothers are listed in a document; there are now only 7 (!) conventuals. From 1200 to 1427 there were only 22 new additions. The shortage of monastery lords had become chronic.[11]

What we still see of the convent in Mittelzell today are only the

---

10 Staiger p. 114
11 Schulte p. 569

remains of the monastery, while most of it was demolished in the 18th century. The monastery was therefore largely empty from as early as 1200, which raises questions about the size of the buildings, the great building activity in the 14th century and its financing. At the time of the Council of Constance in 1415, with its thousands of participants, only two brothers were still on site, and they were unable to prevent entire shiploads of books from being removed from the library.

As more and more wealthy aristocrats joined the monastery as monks, the old wooden church and the convent buildings, which were certainly also made of wood, quickly became too small.

Abbot Wittigo, who is described as being fond of building, therefore erected a new stone Mittelzell church around the year 990 from a full pot of money, including outbuildings such as dormitories, dining rooms, kitchens, washrooms, storerooms, stables for the cattle, workshops, a school, a writing room, accommodation for the servants and guest rooms.

The so-called St. Gallen monastery plan, usually dated to around the year 825 and never realised, almost certainly dates from a much later time. And it is not even entirely certain whether it was created on Reichenau at all.

Dr. Heribert Illig has dealt extensively with this (pseudo) plan[12], and comes to the conclusion with many plausible arguments: "The [St. Gallen] pseudo-plan belongs to the time of 1165 plus or minus 15 years." [Illig 2017, p. 161]

Interestingly, if the plan was created on Reichenau, it was drawn at the same time as the great forgeries of the Reichenau charters. The plan is a fiction of ideas and therefore not an instruction for practical realisation.

One of the arguments against the year 825 and in favour of a later creation of the St. Gallen monastery plan in the 12th

---

12 Heribert Illig: Des Kaisers leeres Bücherbrett, 2017

century is that:

The plan shows a bound measurement system, which only emerged much later. It is the first such architectural drawing, centuries before the next. - However, building history progresses gradually, not in leaps and bounds. The towers shown in the plan are never found in other sacred buildings in Europe before the year 980. The 100 square metre scriptorium shown on the plan is far too large for the early Middle Ages, when there were hardly any books [Illig 1996, p. 246f; Illig 2017, p. 157]

In addition, the plan is completely impractical [Hoffmann 168]. Everything seems far too crowded. The stables for the cattle are right next to the church and the main entrance to the church is only a few metres away from the cattle shed. Why hasn't anyone noticed this yet? The stables, i.e. the lower quarter of the plan, were added by the person who wrote the life of St Martin on the back of the plan. The plan was probably inscribed with the legend of St Martin over a large area on the back so that no one would think of cutting off the added part with the pigsties again. Because this would have destroyed the flow of the text.

One is inclined to think of something like mockery, because who would plan a sheepfold and pigsty right at the entrance to a church? But who would want to mock the Reichenau? The story of St Martin is written on the same parchment, so no one should be tempted to simply throw away the entire plan because of its uselessness or to reuse the parchment.

So is the St. Gallen monastery plan ingenious after all, but in a different way than people generally think? An ingenious mockery of the Reichenau monastery by its greatest adversary, the Serenissima-Venice?

Incidentally, the plan is more reminiscent of a medieval town foundation with its narrow alleyways. However, monasteries have always built on a large scale, with a large inner courtyard - just look at south german abbeys Maulbronn or

Heiligkreuztal.

Where does Reichenau's undisputedly huge property come from?
Historians and village chroniclers always assume a great ruler who gave the extensive property to the monastery as a present, often Charlemagne.
In his chronicle from around 1500, Gallus Öheim assigns the villages to the rulers who are said to have donated them to Reichenau. Here we read of Charlemagne, Karl Martel, Count Gero and others. The village of Göggingen is not listed, although it must have been a rather large settlement in the Middle Ages.
From the lament of Abbot Konrad after the monastery burnt down in 1254, we hear the meaning: What the active hands of honoured princes have gathered for you, Reichenau, these princes are now consuming. They, who called themselves your protectors, have now proved to be robbers in a mad frenzy.
Konrad was close in time to the events, and his lament seems to be authentic. What he says is this: the wealth of the monasteries came from its monastic lords, and the decline was also due to these lords, who had appointed their deputies as administrators (villicus) in the villages. These lords and "royal servants" later turned out to be robbers.

Until now, it was completely unclear how such disproportions could arise. How could the ministerials acquire such power that they were legally able to seize monastic property? It is now quite clear that the ministerials were the deputies of the noble monastic brothers, who sat as stewards on the estates and administered them for their owners, the monastic counts and princes.
The estates therefore appear to have actually remained the property of the nobles, as this would explain the incredible

freedoms and downright insolence of the unruly monks, as well as the obvious fact that the counts and their ministerials were able to sell individual estates in the villages from monastery property into their own pockets. Monastic possession is not necessarily property.

It must be assumed that the extensive land holdings of Reichenau ("from Ulm to Lombardy") originally came from these high-ranking monastic brothers, and they did not call themselves monastery lords for nothing.

In 972, Emperor Otto made a flying visit to Reichenau and dismissed the abbot due to poor financial management.
However, Reichenau must have been flush with money after this, and the new Abbot Bern was able to devote himself to his musical interests from 1008. Shortly before his death in 1048, the newly built St Mark's Basilica, or the so-called Westwerk, was consecrated.
After 1048, when business with the book-illuminations was no longer going well, we see the first signs of an emerging cult of St Mark: for several decades, parts of the relic of St Mark were sold to other monasteries and churches, so-called particles. We do not know how large these particles or parts were. The shrine of St Mark was opened in 1940 and the remains of hip bones, upper arms, vertebrae and other smaller skeletal parts were found. So either the relic was never a complete corpus, or large parts of it were sold as particles in the second half of the 11th century or stolen in the turmoil of the 13th and 14th centuries.

If you look at other monasteries, such as Reichenau's brother monastery of St Gallen, there are a large number of deeds, feudal contracts, books, writings and documents that have come down to us from the Middle Ages. Reichenau, on the other hand, appears to be a veritable desert: only a garden book has survived here, a vision of a monk, a so-called fraternity book in which nothing but 38,000 first names are listed, supposedly the names of all the monks in Reichenau and the wider country. There is also a world chronicle, a few dozen badly forged documents, some contributions to the theory of liturgical chants and a few treatises on mathematics and astronomy.

Gallus Öheim claims that Abbot Eberhard burnt all the old feudal contracts and other documents around 1350. Interestingly, however, Eberhard did not burn the forged documents from the 12th century, as these have been handed down to us. We will return to this idea later.

It is as if Reichenau had been plundered at some point in the Middle Ages, swept clean. But peasants and warriors don't loot documents, they loot supplies. So is cleanliness less a result of military power and more a result of political power? We will also come back to this idea.

The Reichenau monk and monastery teacher Hermann the Lame (+1054) came from a Swabian noble family, was disabled in various ways and could barely speak as a child. Nevertheless, as a later teacher at Reichenau, he mastered the foreign languages Latin, Greek and even Arabic, although Arabic was not a language that had to be mastered from a theological point of view. However, the Arabs were leaders in some areas of science and maths, they already knew the number zero and practised astronomy.

Hermann's qualities and interests were clearly in the field of music and singing, and probably also in the field of astronomy and computistics, i.e. the calculation of annual dates of Easter. A singing teacher who had problems with speaking... It is said that he overcame these problems, which seems possible.

Hermann wrote the so-called Reichenau World Chronicle around 1050. Prof K. Nobbe describes what it is all about:

> However, it has recently been proven by H. Bresslau that up to the year 1043 Hermann used an older work, which Bresslau calls the Swabian World Chronicle; the scanty and clumsy excerpt, which was previously thought to be an excerpt from Hermann's chronicle, also drew from it. ... The sources for the older period are known and this main part of the chronicle has no value for us. The translation therefore only begins with the year 901 ... Finally, from the year 1040 until the year of Hermann's death in 1054, he reported on the events of his own time in a detail that is very different from the brevity of the older part. [Nobbe p. VIII / IX]

K. Nobbe translates Hermann's World Chronicle in his book and only begins this translation in the year 901, as the older part of the World Chronicle is worthless because it has been copied.

Hermann the Lame only writes in more detail about the last 14 years of his life, but forgets to mention a major new building that was constructed before his eyes on the Reichenau. What shall we think about this? The World Chronicle obviously does not have the value that is usually attributed to it.

Arno Borst probably agrees when he writes:

> Reichenau Abbey had never been a centre of historical study since its foundation three hundred years ago. The Reichenau annals were stuck at the year 939.[13]

The Visio Wettini, the vision of the monk Wetti, was probably written around the same time. The abbey must still have been doing well, it must have been in its flowering period, as can be

---

13 Arno Borst: Hermann der Lahme. Hegau - Zeitschrift für Geschichte, Heft 32/33 1975/76

seen from the passage: "It is called Aue, Germany's lands lie all around it, it produces excellent flocks of monks ...".

> Surrounded by deep water
> You rest firmly in love
> Everywhere you spread holy books
> Happy island

Fig.: The famous abbey's garden, painting 1916

However, at the time the Visio Wettini was written, the first moral distortions were probably already spreading: In his vision, Wetti sees various other monks, a former abbot and even a king of Italy[14] sitting in hell and suffering badly there. The purpose of this fictionalised vision should be clear: it is a warning to the monks against misconduct, bad morals and, in particular, greed. After all, greed has always been a particular

14 Charlemagne cannot be meant here, as he never called himself King of Italy.

sin of the noble monks.

> The discipline of monastic life is threatened by many different vices
> Many clergymen, says the angel, eagerly accumulate earthly possessions
> They seek worldly reward at court
> wear fine robes and are not a model of pious living
> They favour sumptuous feasts instead of converting souls
> Seduced by prostitutes, they wallow in their lusts
>
> Be careful, monk, that the Lord does not punish your wealth with hell
> In hell sit monks who purify themselves from sins
> There is a friar who is suffering a harsh punishment
> For he has gathered forbidden wealth
> Monk, you want to be rich, but you were taught poverty
> If you sell Jesus, severe punishment awaits you
>
> We must also severely admonish the monasteries
> They should eradicate the roots of all vice
> Many monks are attached to worldly things
> and only a few come because of God's call[15]

The alleged author of the Visio Wettini is Walafried. He appears to be a fictitious literary figure of Hermann the Lame, just like the alleged first abbot Pirmin[16], whose name was probably chosen by Hermann because of its similarity to his own name.

On the basis of Walafried's information, Hermann the

---

15 Visio Wettini
16 The alleged remains of Pirmin can be found in the Messkirch town church, among other places

Lame thus calculates the year 724 as the year of foundation of the island monastery, and the forgers of the foundation documents adopt this from him; we thus owe the traditional dates for the early history of Reichenau solely to Walafried's tendency to allegorise numbers. The question of which year was the real founding year of the island monastery therefore remains open and must be explained by historians with new conclusions or new methods. [Knittel 19]

Arno Borst's description of Walafried Strabo's life[17] may be nice to read, but it comes across as enthusiastically naive. Of course, you read this biography with completely different eyes when you know that Walafried Strabo never existed, that he is a fictitious character. Let's listen to what Arno Borst has to say about Walafried:

In one of his poems, Walahfrid did not visualise the afterlife, but the future story, as a beautiful book full of rhythmic verse. It was a breathtaking thought, by no means ascetic, but nonetheless monkish, that the poet would capture the earthly world itself in beautiful form through linguistic anticipation. For in the beginning it was the Creator God who had written the book of the world readable, and in the end man made himself noble by freely reaching beyond banal constraints. This was not yet the case. Walahfrid, who had set out to educate people together with many friends, ended up watching the plants grow, in the hope that at some point some flowering dreams would ripen and a few hands would clasp the mighty fruits. [Borst p. 66]

This is Borst's writing style for long stretches: it sounds like maudlin fantasy with no connection to reality.

---

17 Arno Borst: Mönche am Bodensee

The detailed, hidden numerical codes that H. Knittel mentions in his book[18] are strongly reminiscent of Hermann the Lame's computation, because Hermann was well versed in mathematics.

> If we add up the verses dedicated to the two abbots, we get the number 135; if we multiply 135 by 7, we get 945: this is exactly the number of verses in the entire poem ... [Knittel p.17], etc.

Is 945 a reference to a year?

The Reichenau foundation charter of the year 724 has the date 25 April. This alone makes it clear that this document must be a fabrication. It was probably drawn up by Hermann the Lame around 1050 and dated on St Mark's Day (25 April) in 724 of all days, although St Mark only began to play a role on the island 200 years later, around 930. Furthermore, this alleged document by Karl Martel is dated to the birth of Christ:
> 'Written on the twenty-fifth day of the month of April in the year of Christ, when they numbered seven hundred and twenty and four years',

which first became common practice much later, around the year 1000. Before the year 1000, it was regularly dated according to the years of reign, e.g. "in the seventh year of the reign of the Great Karl... ".

In addition to the charter of foundation, Walafried Strabo also appears to be an invention by Hermann: strikingly, he has Walafried entered the monastery as a child, just as Hermann entered the monastery at the age of seven. Is Hermann himself also a fictitious person invented by his alleged pupil Berthold in his Hermann-Vita? We do not know.

―――――――――――――

18 Page 15-18

In any case, the combination of the fortunate circumstances of the time on the one hand, the already moral distortions on the other, the author's good knowledge of Latin, the described greed of the monks and the numerical computerisation of the verses in the book suggest that the Visio Wettini was written in the 11th century, and also suggest that Hermann the Lame himself was the author of the Visio Wettini. These circumstances fit exactly into his time, and only he was able to weave numerical codes into the verses. What the strange numerical references point to, however, is still unclear.

Michael Richter also takes a critical view of the role of Hermann the Lame:
> ... together with the forged foundation charter, these [the sources of Hermann the Lame] were the main sources in the discussion so far, There is a reasonable assumption that the central statement of these sources has no equivalent in reality. [Richter p.18]

Then there is the so-called Verbrüderungsbuch (fraternity book) with its 38,000 name entries. It is unclear why someone went to the trouble of writing 38,000 largely invented names in a book. What is the purpose of this? According to historians, the fraternity book was written when the abbey was 100 years old. However, 38,000 monks could not possibly have lived in the Reichenau monastery during these 100 years, which is why it is assumed that the names of monks from other monasteries were also mentioned in it. If someone wanted to use this fraternity book to demonstrate the size of Reichenau Monastery, then it was pointless. If someone wanted to evoke the spirit of fraternisation between the surrounding monasteries, then this was done with the intention of forgery, because most of the 38,000 people mentioned were certainly purely fictitious.

Very early on, there were disputes and quarrels between Reichenau and the Bishop of Constance over - from today's perspective - insignificant trifles:

> Bern was the abbot who introduced Hermann the Lame to the convent and contributed to the renewed upswing in scholarship and piety. In 1032, Hermann witnessed the fact that the prosperity only lasted as long as the German king and the Bishop of Constance respected the abbey's freedom, and noted it sadly:
>
> "Abbot Bern of Reichenau sent the privileges of his monastery to Rome and again received from Pope John the privilege that he could have church service in episcopal vestments. Inflamed by this, Bishop Warmann of Constance sued him before Emperor Conrad II for usurpation of office and disloyalty.
>
> He was harassed by the two until he handed over this privilege with the sandals to the bishop so that he could 'burn' the privilege publicly at his synod on Maundy Thursday next year. The emperor and bishop thus reduced the solemnity of the Reichenau church service; for Hermann this weighed more heavily than material losses. Conrad II's aversion between 1024 and 1027 also had a detrimental effect on the abbey's property.[19]

The Abbot of Reichenau wanted to be like a bishop, even though he wasn't one, and wanted to compete with the Bishop of Constance. Of course Constance did not put up with this.
One would like to call out to the two quarrellers with Angelus Silesius:

> Friend, arguing is not enough / you must also overcome / Where you want to find eternal rest and eternal peace.[20]

---

19 Arno Borst: Hermann der Lahme. Hegau - Zeitschrift für
    Geschichte, Heft 32/33 1975/76
20 Angelus Silesius: Cherubinischer Wandersmann Volume 6

The Ottonian emperors were the great patrons of Reichenau, and as long as they ruled, the monastery seems to have prospered. In 996, Abbot Wittigo even accompanied the young emperor Otto the Third, whose guardian he was, to the imperial coronation in Rome.

However, when the Salians came to power in 1027, the tailwind began to fade. Business with illuminations went downhill. After the new St Mark's Basilica in Venice was consecrated in 1094 and the cult of St Mark was established there as the state religion, Emperor Henry the Fourth had nothing better to do than immediately travel to Venice and pay his respects to the Doge. Venice had risen to become a world and financial power, and as such it was obviously more important to the emperor's power than Reichenau. Money is important. It was then that Venice began its great political intrigue.

And if you look closely, you can see that it continues to this day. Disintegration and deliberate divisions everywhere, and a monetary system that originated in Venice.

Fig.: Romantic view to the cathedral of Reichenau-Mittelzell, 1891.

Great Power Venice

The Roman writer Juvenal once described conditions in Rome as follows: "The Syrian Orontes has long since flowed into the Tiber". For a long time, Rome considered itself to be morally strong, honest and straightforward. With the conquest of the Orient, immorality, moral decay, superstition and deception, deceit and moral decomposition entered Rome's society, as Juvenal wanted to express with his saying. Social decline came to Rome from the East. Whoever was favoured by power went to Rome, incarnated in Rome. Babylon was no longer the centre of power, no longer Phoenicia, Persia, Egypt or Greece, but Rome.

Then, after centuries of suffering that the Romans had brought upon the world, this empire (western Rome) fell in the 5th century. Rome sank into bloody chaos and the souls of power found a new refuge, a new backdrop in Venice, a city that was well protected from enemy attacks by its lagoon.

Having become immensely wealthy through trade in the 11th century, Venice was involved in European politics from the very beginning, always fearing that the small patch of land on the Adriatic could be wiped out by another great land power.

This is where the Doges developed strategies to ensure their survival. Geostrategy was developed, and how to divide enemy powers and play them off against each other. The Venetians quickly became masters of secret diplomacy, deception and political masquerades. They counterfeited Byzantine coins, manipulated exchange rates, used credit usury and betrayed friends and enemies. It is not for nothing that the mask wearers can still be seen today at the carnival in Venice.

When the Crusaders of the 4th Crusade in 1202 found the land route to Jerusalem too unsafe and arduous, they turned to Venice, which had enough ships to take them to the Holy Land. Although the crusaders had no money to pay, Venice agreed on the condition that the knights recapture the Dalmatian city of Zara for Venice, which they did. The Doge then managed, however, to divert the crusaders from their goal of Palestine and steer them towards Constantinople. There, the crusaders murdered, ravaged and plundered the city and its inhabitants on the Bosporus, Venice's great rival. Large quantities of gold and art treasures were brought to Venice in this way, and Constantinople never recovered from this blow. Even today, the Orthodox Christians have not forgiven the Catholic Christians for attacking and almost destroying them for no reason. Unprovoked? It only seems that way at first glance. For the strongest there is always a reason for war. That is still common political thinking today.

America was discovered in 1492 and the sea route to India in 1498. Venice realised that its land trade with the Orient had seen its best days and was in decline. And in 1509, the European powers of Germany, France, Hungary and others were able to free themselves from the Venetian intrigue and formed the League of Cambrai, which was directed against Venice. Venice spent all the money it could and recruited 40,000 soldiers, but was still defeated. It would almost have been conquered and then incorporated into another principality if the Pope had not withdrawn from the League in 1510.

After this shock, the doges no longer saw any possibility of retaining power in Venice in the long term. Various plans were immediately made for a move, but these were not realised until much later.

Although they were materialists through and through, the rulers at the Rialto realised much earlier and much more clearly that in order to maintain power, it was necessary to control not only matter, but also and especially people's thoughts.

They detested nothing so much as the ideas of the humanists and Nikolaus of Kues that God dwells in every human being, that every human being is animated by a divine spark.
Angelus Silesius later also saw it in the same way as the humanists before him:

> Stop, where are you running to / heaven is within you:
> If you seek God elsewhere / you miss him for and for.[21]

For the devout materialists[22] of Venice, man was only a soulless machine that could be redeemed by his own faith and the grace of God, but never by godly, good and pleasing works. Because good works, as Venice knew of course, were not the goal of his own actions and endeavours. His deeds were anything but pleasing to God.

The humanist and Pope Pius II wrote about the Venetians around 1460:

> They want to appear before the world as Christians, but in reality they never think of God, and apart from the state, which they consider a deity, nothing is sacred to them.[23]

Venice found a great ally who thought the same way: Martin Luther. He also believed that people could only be saved by grace and faith, not by good works.
The great Venetian Cardinal Gasparo Contarini was commissioned to prepare the division of the German church. An empire that is divided and at war with itself is no longer a threat to the lagoon city for a long time. When Luther had to justify himself to princes and the emperor at the council of Worms in 1521, Contarini was also there, sitting next to the

---

21 A. Silesius: Cherubinischer Wandersmann Volume 1 Verse 82
22 this is not a contradiction
23 Comments, p. 743

emperor. Although allegedly on the side of the emperor and the pope, Contarini secretly intrigued in favour of the Reformation. Later, however, he also supported the new Catholic Jesuit order and the Counter-Reformation. He allowed both parties to grow and then set them up against each other. That's how you make truly intelligent politics.

We then see the peak of intelligent rule in the 21st century, where people, completely blinded by propaganda and ideology, are literally begging to be allowed to walk into misfortune themselves. Rulers who are filled with deep awareness try to remain free of karma in this way.
Luther had a close friend without whom the schism would never have happened: Georg Burkhardt. Although largely unknown to the general public, he was undoubtedly the second most important man of the Reformation. Georg Burkhardt called himself Spalatin after his birthplace Spalt near Nuremberg, which means the splitter. Nomen est omen.
Contarini had close connections to the humanist Rufus, and Spalatin was Rufus' pupil.

In a painting by Lucas Cranach the Elder in 1537, Georg Spalatin shows himself with a dishonestly pinched mouth, a false smile and melancholy eyes, eyes that reveal a deep offence he had suffered. Was it because he was exposed to humiliation as an illegitimate child? It must have been his lifelong endeavour to take revenge for an offence, because many years later we still see the same facial expression in another painting. Yet his eyes show no will to power, only a will to change, and overall it is a dishonest face, an agent's face. See appendix.
Spalatin was the chancellor, counsellor, court chaplain, librarian and secret scribe of the Saxon Elector Friedrich der Weise (the wise) and was a Venetian agent. It was Friedrich der Weise, in turn, who held a protective hand over Luther

throughout his life (he died in 1525).

> Luther found the most skilful and understanding advocate for his cause at the electoral court in Georg Burkhardt from Spalt near Nuremberg, who inscribed his name Spalatin in golden letters in the history of the Reformation.[24]

It was Spalatin who organised Luther's escape to Eisenach Castle. Spalatin had a huge quantity of writings printed in Venice, propaganda writings in favour of the Reformation, and had them distributed among the people. There is no doubt about it: Venice wanted to split the church and immediately recognised what propaganda could do to people's minds. It turns people's unconscious outwards, reinforces ideologies and unreal ideas and can ultimately lead to religious wars. This was exactly what Venice wanted.

Venice was later involved in the founding of the Protestant Union in 1608, which led directly to the Great War of 1618-1648.

Of course, Venice did not want the whole of Germany to become protestant. Venice drew its energy from the division and mutual weakening of its enemies, not from their unity.

If we look at Contarini's appearance, we see, like that of Doge Leonardo Loredan, gaunt faces with narrow mouths and eyes full of cool deliberation, gazing into the distance and turned towards a distant target. The target was to retain power, as the Doge's proud and defiant face clearly shows. See appendix.

In the 17th century, Venice moved its centre of power to Geneva, Amsterdam, London and from there overseas. These were the important locations, where there was no confinement for a maritime power, where they founded the East India Company, the Bank of Amsterdam and the Bank of England,

---

24 https://www.luther.de/themen/spalatin.html

and later the Federal Reserve.

Putting aside subjective concepts such as morality, one can speak with great admiration of the rise and millennial rule of Venice over the world and how it still manages to dominate the world by dominating people's thoughts.

Venice was not thrilled that Reichenau was disputing their state saint St Mark. If St Mark lay in the cathedral on the Rialto, who was the one who was venerated in Reichenau? The evangelist was more than a mere symbol for Venice. He was a magical and real[25] guarantor of their power. We see below, in the decline of Reichenau, disintegration, strife, falsification, division and intrigue. And we have to assume that much of this is due to Venice, that all the dispute was fuelled by Venice to damage Reichenau.

The Archaeological Finds in Mittelzell

Archaeological research into Mittelzell Minster first began between 1929 and 1941. At that time, the Constance building director Emil Reisser began excavations in connection with a new heating system that was to be installed.

Reisser died before the printing of his dissertation was completed. It was not until 1960 that his manuscript and drawings were printed, but his original documentation was long considered lost.

> Reisser's publication was much criticised. In 1974, W. Erdmann was able to develop a completely new building history from it - but he was unaware of the original drawings, which were later rediscovered by A. Zettler in the archives of the Hochbauamt (buildings office). [Untermann p.160]
> However, the complete evaluation of the original

---

25 that is not a contradiction

documentation, as well as the exact comparison with the still visible features, based on today's questions, are still pending in Mittelzell and appear to be an important wish for research. [Untermann p.161]

The archaeologists seem to be quite divided!

Despite fierce, but (as we know today) largely unfounded criticism of Reisser's excavations, the opportunity was missed to verify Reisser's results with more modern methods. [Untermann p.158]

Reisser's results appear to be neither unambiguous nor plausible.

In the years 1978 to 1983, Alfons Zettler then examined the west wing of the enclosure in Mittelzell (i.e. not the cathedral). He published the results in his dissertation, which was printed in 1988,

however, without objectifying the excavated contexts and presenting them in detail. His groundbreaking discoveries and new ideas on the history of the construction and use of enclosures and church buildings are therefore not directly verifiable from an archaeological point of view. [Untermann p.161]

There also seems to be great controversy about Reichenau-Oberzell:

In Oberzell, the more recent investigations by Erdmann and Zettler resulted in controversial preliminary reports; the restorative analyses have worsened these controversies. Zettler's archaeological documentation seems to be lost. ... This situation explains why the state of archaeological research on the island of Reichenau is still far from being summarised. ... The finds from

Reisser's and Zettler's excavations have not yet been comprehensively analysed. [Untermann p.163, p.167]

Finally, Abbot Heito/Hatto III (888-913) built a remarkable church in Oberzell, which he had probably initially intended for his burial place. Its early construction history and dating are currently still hotly disputed. [Untermann p.170]

The dating of the famous fresco cycle in the central nave of Oberzell, which depicts the miracles of Christ in eight broadly shown scenes, is also controversial; does it belong to the late 9th century or does it date from the time of Abbot Witigowo in the late 10th century? [Untermann p.170]

Matthias Untermann concludes: "From an archaeological and architectural history point of view, there are admittedly more questions and open problems than answers and certain fixed points - it is not at all easy to say in which buildings the convent lived and celebrated its services at what time. [Untermann p.158]

The reason for this is a "paradox of medieval archaeology", he says. The great density of written records in combination with the large number of excavated building phases makes simple solutions impossible.

Reisser himself identified eight different building phases of the cathedral:

a. The church of the eighth century
b. The new cathedral built by Abbot Heito in 816
c. The extension built by Abbot Erlebald (823-838), a lay church

d. The state of the cathedral in the second half of the ninth century with the pilgrimage church of St Mark
e. The addition of the Chapel of the Holy Cross between 925 and 946
f. Abbot Witigowo's remodelling of the cathedral into a Cluniac unified church in 988-991
g. The rebuilding of the second basilica of St Mark by Abbot Berno in 1048
h. Abbot Diethelm of Krenkingen's cathedral building in 1172.

Reisser writes about these eight construction phases:
> This already provides extraordinarily valuable clues for the assessment of the building finds. They are all the more remarkable as they could be derived purely from the wording of the sources. [Reisser p.22]

This is probably precisely the reason why archaeologists will never agree: namely that the building finds were derived purely from the wording of the sources.

Anyone who believes the fictitious Reichenau miracle stories and the life story of Pirmin, who considers the foundation charter of 724 to be forged (its falsity can no longer be denied), but nevertheless assigns historicity to the events described there, who uncritically follows the reports of Hermann the Lame and Gallus Öheim, i.e. who assumes a monastery building history before the year 900, must inevitably come up against the difficulty of how to distribute too few archaeological finds over a too large period of time.

However, if you cancel Reisser's first four construction phases a to d and replace them with the wooden building from the early 10th century, then everything makes sense again.

Some art historians puzzle over why the side walls in Mittelzell are not decorated with murals, as in Oberzell, and offer the explanation that tapestries must once have hung there. But when Oberzell was built (before the year 1000), painting was still very much in vogue, whereas around 1050, when St Mark's Basilica was built, painting was already in decline. For some reason, the once good business model of book illumination had come to an end, and you may suspect political reasons. The support of the Ottonian emperors had ceased and the Salians were facing headwinds, presumably because of their lenders, the Venetian bankers.

The Decline of the Monastery

In order to be able to understand the decline of the island monastery, we let reports from mostly old books speak for themselves. We do not know whether everything really happened in detail. And as already mentioned, there must have been uplifting days and years. But the old reports give an overall picture that is not overly positive.

What rights the monks took for themselves! And why couldn't the abbots put a stop to the goings-on of their own monks? There can only be one explanation: the monastery was financially dependent on its own friars and priests: the huge monastery property remained the property of the princely monastery lords and the abbey could not dispose of it freely.

In the town Ulm, however, it seemed to be clear: the Reichenauers presented the city of Ulm with a forged document stating that Charlemagne had once donated the city to the island monastery. The forgery was quickly recognised as such by the people of Ulm and they fought tooth and nail against the taxes they had to pay to the distant monastery. But it was not until 1446 that they were completely released from all obligations in return for a payment of 25,000 Gulden. Ulm had therefore not been a gift of property from a princely monk, but it was false, fraudulent monastery property due to a forged document.

However, Reichenau does not appear to have had any real, freely disposable property in the villages. In the later Middle Ages, the princely monastery lords took the right to sell individual farms into their own pockets and to gradually destroy the closed monastery property, the villication. The history books say that the (civil) monastery administrators became powerful for some reason, seized the monastery property and then became nobles themselves.
But this cannot be true, because a commoner could not have ennobled himself. We have to assume that the monastery lords were nobles and had their property administered by unfree ministerials, and that these monastery lords and their ancestors were always entitled to the rights in the villages, and still are. As I said, the situation in Ulm was different.

It was the second birth defect of Reichenau Abbey that, from its foundation until around 1450, it almost exclusively took in brothers from the high nobility. Of course, the abbey quickly became immeasurably rich as a result - but at what later price. The price was dependence on its own friars, who, as nobles, wanted to lead a dissolute, lavish and lordly life, were unable to subordinate themselves and were susceptible to all kinds of financial bribery and influence peddling.
Venice had an easy game.

1080
Under Abbot Ekkehard II (+1088), the monastery was in a sad state. The sciences were in decline, monastic discipline had disappeared, the church was neglected, worship was indifferent and, as in the empire, divisions between spiritual and secular power gave rise to fractions and wars that devastated countries - so there was also discord and confusion on Reichenau. The good times of the monastery,

where piety and brotherly love gave the impulse for everything great and beautiful - they were gone. [Staiger p.112]

1080

The long and terrible fratricidal struggles that devastated the German Empire under Henry the Fourth also affected the monasteries of Reichenau and St. Gallen; the former was loyal to the anti-king Rudolf of Rheinfelden, while the latter was loyal to the emperor. The monks of St. Gallen did not want to put up with Abbot Luitold, who was forced upon them by Rudolf, and broke his abbot's staff when he entered the monastery. He took the hint and renounced his dignity. The emperor now appointed Ulrich, the son of the Duke of Kärnten, as abbot. Abbot Ekkehard of Reichenau believed he had to avenge this disregard for his master and attacked the St. Gallen monastery several times, for which Abbot Ulrich devastated the Reichenau possessions with the war parties provided to him by his father. [Güßfeldt p.51]

1100

It is striking how donations and bequests in favour of the monastery diminished from the beginning of the Crusades. [Güßfeldt p.56]

1130

As a result of the many years of feuding, the prosperity and thus the importance of the abbey had deeply declined; some of its possessions had been pledged and squandered to raise money for the military campaigns. The monastery school had fallen into disrepair, science and art were no longer cultivated and worship was performed without devotion. The long war had brutalised monks and monks' masters; the latter were not afraid to assault and murder a bailiff, a virtuous young man who had come to the island unsuspectingly to worship. In 1135, the monks even killed their own abbot ... [Güßfeldt p.52]

Fig.: Above and below: St Markus Mittelzell.
Centre: St. George Oberzell with the 1000-year-old murals.

1150

... Perhaps it is fair to say that since the death of Hermann the Lame, Reichenau has had no historiographical achievements to show for itself, and even a scriptorium does not seem to have existed there in the 12th century, or only in rudimentary form, if you may conclude this from the few manuscripts of that time that have survived in the Reichenau library. The lack of donations, on which the economic prosperity of an abbey depended, can be explained by comparing the island monastery, which was proud of its nobility and stuck to rigid traditional forms, with the new reform monasteries, in which a lively spiritual and intellectual life prevailed. There, the nobleman could be sure of receiving something in return for his donations: the monks' effective advocacy for him and his family before God and the saints.

The donations to Petershausen, Zwiefalten, St Georgen, Allerheiligen and above all Hirsau make this clear. Powerful monastic life, economic strength, a numerically strong convent and scientific and cultural achievements in the monastery were mutually dependent: at Reichenau in the 12th century, both the one and the other were missing, and so were the copial and tradition book, the founder's chronicle and the monastery chronicle. What should have been described in them for the glory of the present monastery except inner strife and un-monastic behaviour, struggles and economic depression, even poverty. What they had was history, but they had no historian to bring it to life. The rich library, testimony to a great age, fell into disuse, the archive, a storehouse of parchment, remained a pile of raw material for the bookbinder and the forger. [Schwarzmaier p.29]

1180

Diethelm of Krenkingen succeeded in re-establishing discipline and order at Reichenau, improving the monastery school and improving the shattered financial situation;

however, after his death in 1206, a gradual decline set in again, which the circumstances of the time were not able to stop. It can be assumed that the cultivation of the sciences in Reichenau Monastery during the 13th century was as bad as in St. Gallen Monastery, where only one monk could read and write in 1219. [Güßfeldt p.53]

1230

Abbot Heinrich (1206-1234) also presided over the house of God with dignity and blessing. He had the cathedral renovated and repaired, was a friend and promoter of the sciences and even wrote a biography of St Pirmin (Vita St Pirminii). He reigned for 28 years and died in 1234 [Staiger p.113].

1235

Since the monastery fire in 1235, monastic life had rapidly fallen into decline, and the relatively few remaining monks ("monastery lords"), who came from the nobility, lived on their own farms. [Untermann p.168]

1250

Abbot Konrad (1234-1255). This abbot had another bad time. In addition to the discord in the empire, the rebelliousness of the city of Ulm, which was awarded by Emperor Charlemagne to the church of Reichenau, the dispute between Emperor Friedrich II and the popes, whereby the flame and sword of war raged everywhere - the stately and extensive monastery, which once numbered 1600 heads within its walls, burned down in the winter of 1254. [Staiger p.114]

1250

The monastery also owned a manorial property in Ulm with a large pleasure garden, called Grünhof, where 6 or 7 conventuals always lived under a superior. The monastery lords also rode there for tournaments and merrymaking, feasted, drank wine and led such a relaxed life that they caused much annoyance to the citizens of Ulm. What a contemporary writer said about the monks of Reichenau also applied to them: "If someone is lazy and work-shy and wants to live in lavish idleness, he goes to church. There they sit in the taverns, carouse and throw dice and splurge all day long, quarrel and shout in a frenzy of wine, blaspheme God and all the saints and then come out of the arms of their harlots to the altar of God." [Güßfeldt p.63]

1250

The old imperial abbeys had long been home to only a small number of high-born lords, who had little of the true monastic spirit left in them; little by little, each one was able to obtain an office with its assigned income, and the common life and the old monastic discipline fell into disrepair. The abbot became a secular prince, like the others, a rich feudal lord whose direct relations with the monastery were almost completely cut off. [Brandi I p.83]

1254

Extract from Abbot Konrad's lament in 1254 after the monastery fire:
Now come even the insolent, first the royal servants, and fall greedily upon thee. Like common robbers they take what the active hand of honoured princes has gathered for you. And, seeking pleasure, they devour what they have stolen. They, who once proudly called themselves your protectors, have now proved to be robbers in a mad frenzy. [Staiger p.114]

1255

The pious and learned Abbot Konrad was succeeded by Abbot Burkhard [+1259], a baron of Hewen. Under him, the state of the monastery was also still sad. The aristocratic conventuals, accustomed to a lavish life, grew weary and, although Burkhard sold the village of Zurzach to the Bishopric of Constance for 310 marks of silver, he was unable to satisfy them. Burkhard escaped the danger, but the degenerate monastery lords devastated the island in return. [Staiger p.115]

1258

More than war and fire, the lack of discipline among the monks contributed to their decline. They broke out in open outrage as soon as an abbot attempted to restrict their lavish lifestyle. When Abbot Burkhard demanded in 1258 that they put back on their Benedictine robes, which they had long since exchanged for courtly and knightly robes, the monks Friedrich von Thengen and Berthold von Rote decided to murder Burkhard at dinner. The abbot was warned in time and escaped, but the criminal monks gathered armed men, attacked the island, chased away all those who were still loyal to the abbot and plundered the neighbouring monastery estates ... The Bishop of Constance thought this was the right time to take possession of the abbey by force. He raided the island and forced those monks, servants and serfs who had not had time to flee to swear allegiance to him; however, he was forced to abandon the monastery again by order of the Pope. [Güßfeldt p.55]

1312

South of this complex, which was demolished in the 15th century, Abbot Diethelm of Castel built his castle-like abbot's house in 1312 over early and high medieval gravel pits. [Untermann p.168]

1312

Having built new dormitories and dining rooms, the very construction-minded abbot Diethelm III. also wanted to build new lecture theatres for the schools, but met with fierce resistance from the high-ranking monks, who preferred to amuse themselves at the tournaments in Ulm and other festivities rather than play schoolmaster. They feared that the sum set aside for the building would restrict their own lavish lifestyle. Such incidents naturally did not increase Diethelm the Third's popularity with the conventuals, who turned their noses up at him anyway because of his descent from the lower nobility; he therefore preferred to spend the last years of his reign in the fortified tower he had built in Steckborn rather than among his rebellious monks. [Güßfeldt p.57]

1312

Through wilful feuds, unscrupulous administration and senseless waste, Reichenau had become a poor land over the course of a century. Under Abbot Diethelm III., the monastery's income had fallen from 90,000 gulden to 16,000 gulden by the middle of the 14th century; 40 years later, income was only 3 marks of silver. Later, under Abbot Werner von Rosenegg (+1402), the need was so great that he was willing to sell the bones of St Mark to the Venetians, but was forcibly prevented from doing so by the monastery's serfs. The poor Prince-Abbot Werner, of whom Öheim writes that he was a kind and dear gentleman, was finally no longer able to keep his own table; he rode daily at noon and in the evening on his little white horse to Niederzell, where he had given himself cheap board with a priest. [Güßfeldt p.60]

1340

Abbot Diethelm the Third [1306-1343] sought above all to ensure that the monks once again wore the monastic habit according to the Rule of St Benedict, which they had completely abandoned for years. He then built a dining hall, bedrooms and lecture theatres for the schools and ensured that the monastery's income, goods and possessions in Italy, which had been seized in the course of time, had to be returned ... Pope John the 22nd (1316-1334) also ordered that the rights, goods and possessions of the monastery in Germany, which had been lost, should be returned to the monastery -- the high noble monastery lords, on the other hand, who preferred tournaments, jousting at knights' games, making merry at Ulm, going to weddings and feasting, etc., instead of occupying themselves with church, religion and science - the austere lesser noble abbot was not at all pleased. In order to escape from their arrogance, Diethelm built a solid and massive tower for himself in Steckborn, the castle. There he lived quietly and yet close to the abbey until death took him 1342. [Staiger p.118]

1350
Enmity began, which lasted over seven years and in which the lords of Brandis on Reichenau also took part. Their first hostile act was against fishermen in 1366, when the cellar master Mangold von Brandis and the cantor of the monastery went on a pleasure cruise. They came across a fisherman from Petershausen who had crossed the borders of the district and was fishing in the abbot's territory. They immediately approached him and gouged out his eyes. The blind man was taken to the council chamber in Constance. The citizens were so outraged by the sight of him that they hurriedly sent troops to burn and destroy the farms of those lords on the Au. [Staiger p.122]

In 1368, however, one story turned out very badly. It was between Christmas and Shrove Tuesday, when 27 citizens of Constance wanted to go to Zurich for a jousting match. Abbot Eberhard von Brandis also sent 27 men there with his two relatives Wölfle and Thüring von Brandis.
When the two sides met at Bassersdorf, those from Reichenau immediately charged at those from Constance and stabbed five of the horses. The Constans then attacked the

Reichenauers, stabbed Wölfle von Brandis, who lay dead in the field, and took four prisoners. Thüring now fled with the rest.

Afterwards in the same year the market ship sailed from Constance to Stein to market. Abbot Brandis and his men stood on guard under Neuenburg Castle [near Mammern] at night. When the ship arrived, they sailed towards it, boarded it, drew their weapons and stabbed nine servants. Others were wounded and all were left lying in the ship. The ship turned back. The matter came before the council and the people of Constance immediately set off for Marbach [on Untersee] with 18 ships, conquered the fortress [which belonged to the Reichenau cellar master Brandis] and burnt it together with the stables. Nine servants were also captured; they were taken to Constance and had their heads cut off at the place of judgement near the large stone at Kreuzlingen. [Staiger p.124]

In 1370, the citizens of Constance destroyed the hated Schopfeln Castle, which has stood in ruins at the entrance to Reichenau ever since, due to another act of violence committed by the Brandis family against Constance fishermen. Previously, the abbot had borrowed money from Bishop Ulrich III (+1351), and when this was wasted, it went back to mortgaging and selling. [Staiger p.125]

1360

Since unworthy abbots, especially those of Brandis [1343], presided over the monastery, all evil has moved into the monastery walls. The many journeys of the gracious lords brought foreign customs and opulence into the monastery; the wanton feuds and wastefulness exhausted the treasures; the dissolute economy deprived the abbey of goods and income; the travelling of the monastery lords to tournaments, carnival games, weddings and dances alienated the noble lords from their spiritual profession. Discipline was relaxed, good manners corrupted, luxury took the place of frugality, and the monastery became a place of indulgence - church and library abandoned. ... under the Brandis', the annual pensions were barely three marks of silver or 72 florins. When Abbot Werner von Rosenegg took over the abbey, the monastery was completely impoverished; he no longer had enough to set his own table. [Staiger p.129]

1390

In times of great need, Abbot Werner von Rosenegg (1385 to 1402) had to move, pledge and sell many things; however, when he wanted to hand over St Mark's to the Venetians, he was prevented from doing so by the servants [the serfs]. The poor abbot died on 24 April 1402 [Staiger p.130].

1428

When Abbot Friedrich, Baron of Wartenberg, assumed his dignity in 1428, he found only two novices in the monastery, Heinrich Count of Lupfen and Hans Baron of Roseneck; all the others had left before his arrival, as the reputation of a zealous, austere man preceded him, some to their homes, others to the war against the Appenzellers. The abbot then told the two friars that from then on they would have to live strictly according to St Benedict's rule. [Gußfeldt p.62]

1430

It was not until Abbot Friedrich II. of Wartenberg (abbot from 1427-1453) that Reichenau Abbey began to shine again. His election took place in 1428 and when he took over the abbey, two novices were still in the monastery. The others went up and away: some home, others to the armies against the Appenzellers, - and finally the two novices also left, for they lacked the inner urge for monastic life, the warm heartfelt desire for quiet solitude, that humility and piety which only has joy in the church and the cell, the true earnestness for a union with God. What drove them to the monastery were completely different reasons.

They believed they could lead a pleasant, comfortable, free, unbound life here; hence the reluctance, the displeasure, the unhappiness, the annoyance - when the abbot set them a modest table, insisted on the observance of monastic discipline and urged them to attend church punctually. After all, monastic life, when practised properly, is not as pleasant and beautiful as is usually believed: prayer has its hours, rest has its time, everything has its limits. Sometimes Matins calls, sometimes Prim, Terce, Sext, Non, Vespers and Complet, sometimes the confessional prayer, and - while the layman can rest at night - the bell calls the monks to the choir at midnight. Therefore, anyone who does not feel a real calling to monastic life and only enters the inviolable threshold of the monastery for earthly reasons and with earthly desires and passions - will not find the peace he hopes for there. In order to dedicate oneself to God and the Church, one must therefore be fulfilled and imbued with it. Failed hope, destroyed love, offended vanity, expectation of a delightful life must never open the monastery door - otherwise bitter remorse will follow; but for those whose desires are satisfied and become one with the covenant of the Church, the monastery will be an place of refuge, a place of contentment, a joyful and happy home. [Staiger p.131/132]

1440

In the meantime, the monestary was inhabited by a few monks sent to it by the Abbot of St Blasien, until it was populated anew. Of course, princes, counts and dukes no longer came to the monastery, but many from the lower nobility were admitted since the abbot Friedrich granted this admission. In 1437, Friedrich had the monastery surrounded by a wall and new monastery halls and rooms built, as well as a new roof on the bell tower, as the old one had been blown down by a storm.

1446

In 1446, after a lengthy trial and a 14-year excommunication of the people of Ulm, the abbot [Friedrich] sold the remaining rights, dues and privileges that the monastery had in Ulm to this town in return for 25,000 gold gulden, thus freeing Ulm completely from the Reichenau church. [Staiger p.135]

1490

For those to whom the word of the pope is proof, the bull of Pope Innocent the 8th removes all doubt. In this papal bull it is said: That the body of St Mark really rests in Reichenau and awaits the last day of judgement there, and that he promises indulgence for ten years to those who make a pilgrimage to his holy relics. [Güßfeldt p.19].

1540

Abbot Markus treacherously agreed to hand over the abbey to the bishop in return for a large settlement. The handover took place on 6 February 1540. Markus, who was physically and mentally weakened by a stroke and perhaps not fully aware of his dishonest behaviour, was promised an annual life annuity of 1,400 gulden, 10 barrels of wine and 20 fathoms of wood, as well as a house in Radolfzell and one in Bohlingen; On his departure, in addition to what he had been promised, he was given all of the monastery's silverware (with the exception of 8 mugs), 12 carboys of wine [1 carboy is 12 buckets], a large supply of grain, 10 complete beds, 2 dinner services and his personal horse. As he was travelling across the water to Radolfzell with his booty, a storm arose that was so violent that the ship threatened to capsize. He moved into his house in Radolfzell, held court there and died after 9 months. [Güßfeldt p.67]

1540

Thus ended a monastery, writes Staiger in his book about Reichenau, which for several centuries was a fertile mother of holy and pious men, a school of knowledge and science - a monastery in which for a long time only princes, dukes, counts and barons were allowed to be admitted as capitulars - a monastery to which popes and emperors bestowed their favour and grace to a greater extent [...] - a monastery that was one of the richest monasteries in Alemannia thanks to its numerous endowments and which, with its blessed island, could rightly call itself Reichenau (the rich Au) - a monastery that had such extensive landholdings that legend still tells of it today: When the abbot of Reichenau travelled to Rome, he was able to stay overnight on his own land every day - a monastery that once had 300 noble vassals and from which 4 archdukes, 10 palatine counts and margraves, 27 counts and 28 barons and knights held fiefs. [Güßfeldt p.68]

1550

In his cosmography published in Basel in 1550, Stumpf reports on this controversial matter: "The evangelist St Mark is also said to be alive in this monastery, which is why the monks have not sung or read St Mark's Gospel Secundum Marcum, but secundum illum, which the Venetians have not endeavoured to do a little, Venice have wanted to give them a large sum of money for it, but the monks have not wanted to do so". [Güßfeldt p.18].

Stumpf's cosmography thus says: Because the Reichenau monks insisted on their claim to uniqueness with regard to their island saint, the Venetians made great efforts to buy the relic from Reichenau for a large sum of money. But the monks did not want to sell it.

Despite the obvious powerlessness of the Reichenau abbey leadership, or perhaps because of it, the extent of the dispute is remarkable. For years and decades, a pointless dispute was fought to the death with Constance over trivial matters, which led to great devastation on the island.

> "They are fighting, it is said, for freedom rights;
> but to be precise, they are servants against servants".[26]

From today's perspective, the reasons for the dispute were trivial, but for contemporaries at the time they were probably existential. The diocese of Constance wanted to incorporate Reichenau and the abbey fought tooth and nail.
But didn't the abbey originally have a spiritual, christian, missionary goal? This seems to have been completely forgotten in the course of the High Middle Ages.

The great fire of 1254 may not have broken out by chance, but was probably started on purpose. All the deeds and other documents may not have simply disappeared, but were stolen and destroyed. One is inclined to see a great troublemaker: Venice. Because of the double St Mark, Venice had a great interest in keeping Reichenau small. The entire moral decomposition of the monastery is unthinkable without an external cause. The Bishop of Constance and the Abbot of Reichenau, who were still working together harmoniously at the time of foundation, were successfully divided after 1100.
Abbot Diethelm had new, larger buildings erected in the early 14th century, and one wonders where the money came from. The abbey was already in free fall at the time. But a financial power like Venice was always prepared to lend money to its opponents (everyone was its opponent), which was later reclaimed with compound interest and drove the opponent to ruin.
Around 1340, the Venetian banks went bankrupt because they had granted too many non-repayable loans, and a major financial and economic crisis developed that affected the

---

26 Johann Wolfgang von Goethe

whole of Europe and led to the Great Plague of 1349. This put Abbot Eberhard von Brandis (+1379) under so much pressure that he had to sell almost all of Reichenau's assets, whatever they were. In his distress, he sold it to his own relatives.

Historians criticise the poor financial management of this abbot of difficult character and the fact that he sold off property and possessions on a grand scale, but fail to realise that he certainly had no choice. The creditor was breathing down his neck, and that could only have been Venice, because Venice had built up an extensive banking and financial network across Europe, more extensive than that of the Knights Templar.

Jealous Venice

In 1428, the new Abbot Friedrich von Wartenberg arrived on the island, "the new Pirmin", as Gallus Öheim and Conrad Gröber called him.

He managed to steer the abbey's affairs back onto a more or less orderly course. When he took up his post, there were only two novices left in the monastery, they were relatives of him; because Friedrich was regarded as a strict lord, all the others had left beforehand, off to war campaigns against the Appenzells or elsewhere. And these two novices did not stay for long, so we read, so that Frederick soon had to borrow some monks from St. Blasien if he did not want to live alone in the monastery. In 1437, he had a wall built around the abbey, built new halls and rooms and had the church and furnishings extensively renovated from the middle of the 15th century.

One wonders what the point of all this new building activity was, given that the monastery was apparently only inhabited by a few monks. But Friedrich, not wanting to live alone in the monastery, opened the convent to the lower nobility, and so the monastery probably filled up again. Instead, the high nobility stayed away. Nothing was more important to people in the Middle Ages than origin and class distinction.

Friedrich died in 1454, and under his successor, Johann of Hinwil, the old bad relationships immediately resumed. Johann was unable to assert himself in legal matters and was in serious conflict with his convent at the end of his 10-year term of office. In 1457 he had a monk imprisoned and five years later some monks left the monastery in protest.

Under Abbot Johann Pfuser (1464-1491), the cult of St Mark was then publicly intensified and revitalised. The late gothic tomb of St Mark was probably erected during his early term of office. In 1477, the cathedral was reconsecrated and St Mark was officially elevated to co-patron of the cathedral:

> The double patronage of "St Mary and St Mark" was first recorded in the professed formula in 1442 and has been predominant since 1454. This repeatedly postulated special status of St Mark was finally officially confirmed with his elevation to co-patron saint in 1477. [Bock]

St. Mark's tomb in cathedral Reichenau-Mittelzell.

Why did St Mark finally become a church patron so late, only after centuries? This is a remarkable fact, and one must assume a headwind in favour of it.

Abbot Pfuser's decrees of 1465, 1473 and 1486 can be understood as advertising measures for the veneration of the evangelist, which were intended to bring money into the monastery's coffers. Pfuser also gave private groups of visitors the opportunity to view the relic of St Mark, presumably for a high fee.

From 1473, Pfuser even minted his own coins, the so-called Reichenauer Rollbatzen, with St Mark as the image on the coin. And from the year 1500, we have Radolfzell coins with the inscription Moneta Augie maioris and St Marcus Evangelista. These coins even show the image of the winged lion of St Mark.

They are so-called bracteates, i.e. pieces of metal stamped on one side with no actual value.[27] An expression of Reichenau's financial hardship, or forgeries by Venice?

Venice was not thrilled by any of this. Just one year later, in 1474, the Venetian cardinal and legate Marcus Barbo paid a visit to Reichenau. He was received with great honour and shown all the holy relics such as the jar from the Wedding of Kana, the Holy Blood of Christ and the church treasures. When he was finally shown the most important relic, the shrine of St Mark with his bones, Barbo inspected the shrine from the outside and saw St Mark in relief with the lions, saw the scene on the shrine where the Venetian swore to the authenticity of the relic with the cauldron catch, also saw the four lions of St Mark holding the shrine, and perhaps also saw the winged lion of St Mark on the gable of the entrance to the altar chamber of the former high altar.

---

27 see Dr O. Roller: Die Münzen der Abtei Reichenau. in: Die Kunst der Reichenau vol. 1. p. 540

Fig.: Winged lion of St Mark with book, on the entrance to the altar chamber in Reichenau-Mittelzell (1477).

By then he had seen enough and snubbed the abbot with an unparalleled affront, suddenly showing no further interest in the bones and not wanting to see them at all. Another source says that Barbo wanted to see the bones but then simply left before the shrine was open.

> Both versions share a remarkable lack of interest in the bones of St Mark the Evangelist for a Venetian-born papal legate and cardinal of San Marco Evangelista al Campidoglio - the Roman regional church of Venice: the refusal of the extraordinary honour, apparently only granted to visitors of the highest rank, of being allowed to see the relic in person and even touch them. [Bock]

You can clearly recognise the Cardinal's mood, as well as that of Venice. The affront was intended to make the people of Reichenau understand what Venice thought of the flaring cult of St Mark and is to be understood as a kind of warning. But the people of Reichenau were not sensitive enough to recognise this.

When Constance citizen Konrad Grünenberg made a pilgrimage to Jerusalem in 1486, he also passed through Venice and described the Venetian churches and their relics, church treasures and furnishings in detail. But Grünenberg does not mention the highest shrine, the relic of St Mark, in his report.

Six years later, on 5 September 1492, a group of several visitors from Venice arrived on Reichenau from Strasbourg. The group had met with Emperor Ferdinand in Strasbourg and was on its way back to Venice. Thanks to the report of the 20-year-old Andrea de Franceschi, who was travelling with them, we know how the travellers fared on Reichenau. They were shown many relics of saints and in particular a silver box adorned with stones and gems and other similar silver boxes with saints inside. There were also relics of the thorns of Christ, of the wood of the cross and the blood of Christ, of the milk of the Virgin Mary, the body of St Fortunatus, the bones of St Stephen, St Isidore, St John and St Paul and many beautiful devotional crosses with precious stones and carnelians of the greatest beauty.

However, Franceschi does not mention the Kana jar, the emerald and the highly holy relic of St Mark in his report, which is all the more striking in view of the fact that the group of visitors came from Venice.

The Dominican and researcher Felix Fabri (+1502) questioned the authenticity of the relic of St Mark: either there must have been two Marks, or St Mark must have had two bodies.

On the other hand, there never seems to have been a real controversy on this issue in the sense of an ongoing or repeatedly revitalised debate between representatives of Venice and those of Reichenau, as the comments of various authors of the 17th and 18th centuries suggest. [Bock].

What should they have discussed? Both knew that both relics were fake, and each knew that the other knew this too.

The revival of the cult of St Mark at the end of the 15th century clearly did not benefit Reichenau. On the contrary: a few years later, in 1508, there were once again only two lonely monks in the abbey. However, we do not know by what means Venice brought about the renewed decline of the island abbey.

The Medival Village of Göggingen

A villication is a manorial form of living together in an early medieval village. A genuine villication is characterised by the following features:

- An institution or a ruler holds the so-called lordship, i.e. the institution is recognised as the authority in the village. This lord of the manor determines rights, duties, laws, penalties and taxes.
- All property in the village belongs to this landlord or this institution, e.g. a monastery.
- The institution, subsequently referred to as 'the monastery', can administer justice and impose penalties.
- The peasants are in bondage, i.e. they do not work for their own account, have no decision-making power, but work on instruction.
- A villication is self-sufficient, which means that craftsmen must live in it as well as farmers.
- All yields go into a common pot, from which the monastery then takes the surplus.
- The monastery propagates a village community, a so-

called familia.
- Help is granted to residents in need.
- A villication is not based on the free will of its inhabitants but on coercion.
- The lord of the manor does not live in the village personally but appoints a local administrator.

First there was the monastery, then came the villication.

Villication is a completely new form of economic activity and coexistence. It did not exist before in antiquity. In Roman times, farms were subject to an annual tax, and how the farm owner earned this tax was his own business. The administrative effort involved was high, as each farm had to be recorded and accounted for individually. Later, when villication fell apart in the Middle Ages and the farmers' income no longer went into a common pot, the system was switched back to a tax-based economy, which proved to be more stable and practical.
Villication was therefore only a brief interlude in the early Middle Ages, an attempt to minimise administrative costs by creating small communist economic units.

Monasteries in particular must have regarded villication as the ideal form of living together, think of St Benedict and his rules for monks living together. The idea of villication is modelled on these rules.
There can only be one landlord in a village, but there are many farms in a village, all of which can have different owners. The idea of a villication was to prevent this fragmentation of ownership, but it quickly failed in this task.
The crucial point of a villication is of course: by what right could a villication be established? Who gave the landlord the right to a village? They say a great man, an emperor or a count. That is conceivable. But even more interesting is: how

were the peasants' houses and fields expropriated? After all, the germanic peasants of the Migration Period were still free, or at least always referred to as such.

How did the nobles come to own the personal property of the peasants in a villication? A ruler can claim lordship, but not private property.
Unfortunately, the sources are silent on these points.

A villication suffers from various things: Bondage and involuntariness make it ineffective. Houses and estates fall apart if they do not belong to the farmer and the owner does not live in them.
Early on, individual farms in a villication were sold, which means that there were increasingly farms that operated differently, that did not contribute anything to a common pot, that could place themselves outside the villication community, whose higher performance was reflected in the form of greater prosperity.
As more and more farms were virtually cut out of the villication early on, the villication quickly began to disintegrate. This accelerated when the first towns were founded, from around 1120 onwards, and the farmers in a villication literally fled to the neighbouring towns to escape the communist lack of freedom and wealth in the villication. This signalled the end of the villication economy, the 'common pot' was abolished and the tax economy began. Each house was then subject to an individual annual tax, which had to be paid to the respective owner.

It can be seen that all of the above characteristics must always be fulfilled at the same time for a genuine villication to exist. The mixed forms of villication that emerged, some with private property ownership, did not last long, but quickly brought the villication constitution to an end.

Also political socialism in the 20th century could only become communism if all countries were brought into line; no country was allowed to be capitalist, there should be no room for manoeuvre. At least that is how the Marxists themselves saw it in their own theory.

In any case, like communism, the idea of vilication failed due to its own ideology, which did not correspond to reality.

It is fair to assume that Göggingen was once a Reichenau village. This can be seen in the Diethelm charter from 1202, where a "Bertoldus villicus de gegingen" is listed. And we also read the place name "gecgingen" in the Reichenau Walafried document, which was written between 1142 and 1165. Due to the size of the village of Göggingen, one might have expected this document to list more levies to be paid to the monastery, but this document is one of the many forgeries of Reichenau documents, whose content was falsified anyway.

The connection to Reichenau can perhaps still be seen in the field name Auerrain and can certainly be seen in the probably largest and oldest building in the centre of the village, today's Adler inn, which was once a manor house in Reichenau times.

This can also be seen in a large number of local feudal deeds from the second half of the 14th century, when the abbots Brandis, Pfuser etc. granted fiefs to various local farmers. And it can be seen even more clearly in the large sales of estates in the 14th and 15th centuries, when the farms of the former villication were sold on a large scale to foundations, wealthy townspeople, private individuals, knights, squires and other lower nobility in the neighbourhood.

The Gögginger Dorfbuch (chronicle) [=GD] writes about the beginnings of the Villikation:

   There must have been a great one behind the donation

of Göggingen, for the farms and estates granted here were so extensive, in contrast to the surrounding area, that Göggingen became a villication, i.e. that a Reichenau estate administration was established here and the Reichenau Kelnhof was a place of judgement. Göggingen was under the dominion of the Reichenau Imperial Abbey and was administered by the Villicus or Meier, to whom the Cellerar or Kellermeister was subordinate. The peasants belonging to the villication were under the leadership of this Kellermeister. [GD p.14]

Unfortunately, there are no feudal documents for Göggingen before around 1350, as Abbot Brandis is said to have burnt all these documents, at least according to Gallus Öheim in the early 16th century.
From what can be reconstructed, Reichenau had dominion over Göggingen, and had ownership or property rights as well as lower jurisdiction. It is very likely from the extent of these possessions that Göggingen was once a genuine villication, i.e. there was no private property ownership by the peasants at that time. As already mentioned, it is unclear how the peasants could have been dispossessed when law and contracts were of such paramount and binding importance throughout the Middle Ages.

Hardly anything is known about the formation of the Gögginger villication, but we do know about its gradual dissolution. Let the Göggingen village book speak for itself:
The more the power and wealth of the abbey declined in the course of the Middle Ages, the more influential and independent these servants of the monastery became, who were able to acquire more and more property and rights as the monastery lost property and influence, until they became the actual lords of the villication and their

service to the monastery changed to knightly allegiance during feuds and military campaigns or the emperor's journeys to Italy, for which the monastery had to provide armed horsemen (knights) and crew. The villicus thus became the ministerial, the noble servant, knight or squire. [GD P.14]

But a peasant villicus could not become a nobleman "just like that". The class system in the Middle Ages was impermeable and did not allow such social advancement.

After the nobles of Geggingen, the Knights of Hohenfels came into possession of our village [around 1300]. The former united Reichenau estate of the Göggingen villication was already torn apart and fell into different hands. [GD P.16]

We hear about our mill in Göggingen as early as 1330, when the landlord and owner was Reichenau Monastery. When the island monastery declined economically, the mill first fell to the local Reichenau ministerials, the Maier von Geggingen, and from them the village and mill came into the possession of the Lords of Hohenfels. [GD P.153]

The Adler inn was apparently once the seat of the Meier von Göggingen, i.e. originally the administrative building of the Reichenau villication, the monastic estate in Göggingen. After the Meier von Geggingen became the actual owners of the village, the house served as a manor house for these noblemen (ministerials). The location and building also indicate the old manor house. [GD P.189]

It can be assumed that the ministerials did not come into

possession of village property "just like that", but bought it from their noble monastery lords. It is impossible that in the Middle Ages a peasant, a ministerial or an insignificant nobleman could take away possession of a monastery property.

> There is documentary evidence that the beneficiaries of Reichenau's losses were its ministerials. The impoverished monastery no longer had the power to defend itself against the desire of its knights and yeomen, who sat as stewards on the Reichenau manors and estates, and so these servants of the manorial lordship were promoted in large numbers to knights and ministerials, into whose hands fiefs, titles and other rights of the monastery passed. [GD p.224]

However, servants and peasants could not be promoted to knights and ministerials.

> In the case of Göggingen, the ownership of the Göggingen Villicus family in 1330 still shows us this transition from a reichenau estate to private ownership, and there is no doubt that the lords of Hohenfels also brought together their large estate in Göggingen in the period around 1300 from original monastery property. [GD p.136]

In the search for the person who brought Göggingen to Reichenau, one comes across the Counts of Pfullendorf:

> Of the powerful count dynasties there, there is no evidence of the Counts of Heiligenberg and their successors, the Counts of Werdenberg (since 1298) on Reichenau, but there is evidence of the von Nellenburg and von Pfullendorf dynasties. This family, which died out in 1105, provided the oldest monk and abbot, whom

we name after his family, Abbot Eckehard (1071 to 1088); the family Nellenburg-Veringen is not represented. Abbot Ludwig (1131-1135), who was murdered in Tuttlingen, came from the Pfullendorf family (extinct after 1180). [Schulte p. 558]

It therefore appears that the village of Göggingen came into the possession of Reichenau through Count Rudolf of Pfullendorf (1110-1181), or probably through one of his predecessors. This happened in the 11th or 12th century. Rudolf's ancestral seat was Ramsberg Castle near Großschönach, which was sold to the Überlingen hospital in 1409. Rudolf's only son Berthold (*around 1150) died in 1167 during Emperor Barbarossa's fourth Italian campaign. Count Rudolf himself war the cousin of emperor Barbarossa.
However, these counts of Pfullendorf and their direct and indirect descendants never lived in the village, but in a town or castle in keeping with their rank, and had the village of Göggingen administered by a non-free ministerial (villicus). There is therefore much to suggest that Ramsberg Castle was once the seat of the dominion of Göggingen.

The Göggingen village book also recognises connections to Pfullendorf and Überlingen:
> It is very likely that the von Geggingen family left their original home around 1300 and settled in two separate branches of the family in Überlingen and Pfullendorf. Because in 1330, Pfullendorf patricians negotiated a manor in Göggingen, which they called "Werner the Geggingener's property".

But one can assume, contrary to the statement in the village book, that the "von Geggingen" had always lived in Pfullendorf and belonged to a collateral line of the Count of Pfullendorf.

After the Pfullendorf male line died out, Göggingen was later sold to the Hohenfels family, which would mean that Reichenau could not dispose of the Göggingen property, but that many property and land rights always remained with the Pfullendorfers.

When the number of aristocratic monks declined sharply in the 12th century, the monastery became impoverished because the noble families reclaimed their property back from Reichenau.

Even later, any remaining influence of the Reichenau was increasingly lost and became almost insignificant:

> In 1446 we find the main part of the Reichenau estate at Göggingen in the hands of the noble lords Albrecht and Ortolf von Heudorf, who held this property in fief from Reichenau Monastery, but disposed of it freely when they sold it to Überlingen patricians on 1 July 1446. The fact that this sale was the centrepiece of the Reichenau villication is evident from the fact that the Kelnhof, the mill and the storage barn are listed among the estates sold. A total of 17 estates are mentioned with the names of their feudal farmers. It is indicative of the insignificance of their reichenau origin that there is not a word to indicate the consent of this supreme feudal lord. [GD p.137]

The deed of sale made no reference to the consent of the supreme feudal lord.

At that time, however, no feudal tenant could sell property belonging to the feudal lord into his own pocket, just as today no tenant can sell his landlord's farm, and no tenant can sell his landlord's flat. We must therefore assume that the properties sold were the property of the seller and not the property of Reichenau.

The administrators of the Villikation Göggingen of
Reichenau Monastery during the Carolingian period
(around 800) were free farmers who lived on the
Reichenau monastery estate (Kelnhof). Initially a monk
was probably the steward in Göggingen, until the
decision of an abbots' synod in 816 forbade this and
demanded that free peasants should take over this
office. [GD p.14]

It may have been different: the synod in Aachen in 816 never
took place and the resolutions, which mainly concern the sole
acceptance of Benedict's rules, are fictitious. They are later
inventions from a time when the villication was already in
serious decline, i.e. in the 12th century. It had become too
uncomfortable and unsafe for the monasteries to have their
own noble monks as administrators in the villications. They
wanted to get rid of them and replace them with peasants or
ministers, which is probably why these alleged synodal
resolutions were invented.
However, the fraud had no effect, because when the villication
was still alive, peasants were never its administrators. That
would make little sense. Only much later, when the villication
was torn apart, when it was divided into many different
owners, with no 'common pot' anymore, did yeomen end up
as administrators, the forerunners of the mayors.

Of the large original Reichenau property, we only find 8
estates in the Gögginger Urbar book of 1686, which are
Reichenau property [GD p.140]

By 1744, only 1.2% of the former extensive Reichenau
property in Göggingen remained.

It is often said that the monastery became weak and because

of this weakness, the ministerials then seized the monastery property. But it seems more likely that many noble monks left the monastery from the 12th/13th century onwards due to the impossible conditions there, reclaiming their family's estates when they left, which they had often 'leased' to Reichenau for economic use a long time ago, and the monastery became then impoverished as a result.

The sin-less Au became the rich Au, then the sin's Au, and then the poor Au.

The Reichenau Forgery Workshop

The fact that Reichenau had a forgery workshop in the 12th century is nothing new. Researchers discovered this 150 years ago. Around the year 1150, dozens of fabricated documents were produced in the Reichenau scriptorium, some of which were then used as models for other monasteries, many of which also practised forgery. The aim was almost always to gain some kind of advantage by referring to old property that the monastery allegedly had in previous centuries.

Two things can be recognised: firstly, the absolute faith that the villages had in a written parchment. However, this respect only worked among the uneducated peasant villagers, where nobody could write and where nobody could defend themselve legally; but in towns like Ulm there were lawyers and councillors who immediately doubted such fabrication and took action against it, as the people of Ulm did against the Reichenau.

Counterfeiting had no direct effect on bishops and kings, however, as they were aware of the practice of counterfeiting and forged documents themselves. Here it was important to forge particularly well and credibly.

On the other hand, we can see that the Middle Ages were not

a legal vacuum. On the contrary: you could pull out a centuries-old contract and your opponent could not simply reject it because of its age. Treaties were valid, no matter how old they were. In principle, this is still the case today.

Even the most famous and largest forgery in world history, the Constantinian Donation, had an effect for centuries by falsely granting the popes a Papal State, "half of Italy" and thus a secular power, which these 'representatives of God' were able to use for their power politics until the 19th century. However, the forger of this alleged donation, which was probably invented in the 11th century, made a serious mistake by referring to Byzantium as Constantinople, which was still completely unusual in the early 4th century. In 330, Byzantium was initially renamed Nova Roma and only received the name Constantinople after Constantine's death in 337.

All researchers assume that the creation of false documents brought the forger some kind of advantage. Why else would he have gone to the trouble of exposing himself and his monastery to accusations of unseriousness? However, the opponents who were to be harmed by the forgeries were suspicious and had advisors and lawyers who, of course, took suspicious ownership claims to court immediately.

The fact that various Reichenau forgeries did not benefit the monastery, but were actually created with the intention of harming the monastery, will become clearer when we look at the documents of the village Göggingen.

On the surface, Reichenau's opponent was the Bishopric of Constance, which wanted to incorporate the island abbey. We do not know with what justification. However, most monasteries certainly emerged from a diocese, i.e. they were founded by the diocese, in the case of Reichenau probably by the diocese of Constance. It can therefore be assumed that the diocese had legitimate but unverifiable rights to the island monastery.

The island, which had become wealthy, then generated covetousness in Constance. The situation was complicated by the fact that the external property of the monastery was probably not its property at all, but belonged to the monastery friars.

Incorporation into Constance would have meant the end of the monastic business model: the wealth of the monastery in exchange for monastery lords who were allowed to live the life of lords. So, incorporation would have immediately impoverished the monastery.
In the years between around 1080 and 1122, the Investiture dispute raged in Germany. The emperor and the church fought over unclear ownership claims. Who owned the monasteries, who owned the external possessions of the monasteries, what jurisdiction should apply there?
Because the monasteries were located on imperial territory, imperial law was to apply there and imperial bailiffs were to administer justice. This jurisdiction by the bailiffs remained unclear for a very long time.

But at least the dispute over ownership was settled in 1122 at the Concordat of Worms: Property that the church could prove had been donated to it in the past was allowed to remain with the church or the monastery. Former women's property also remained untouched and was thus excluded from the imperial assets.
The ink was barely dry on the text of the concordat, the first forgeries began, which were intended to document donations in the distant past. It was regularly recorded that a fictitious emperor, count or prince had given this or that to the monastery a long time ago. Or, more rarely, that some fictitious women had once owned the monastery long before.

Gerhard Anwander has investigated this in more detail using

the monastery of Neustadt am Main, which resisted incorporation by the Bishop of Würzburg:

> ... For this purpose, people are invented from scratch, such as a sister of Charlemagne. Or invented persons such as Pippin, Megingaud, Charlemagne and Count Hatto are used as founders. Prominent and also invented saints such as Boniface and Willibald are allowed to decorate the fictitious foundation ceremony of the monastery in order to enhance its value; and real people such as Otto III. are also used by forging documents for them - the latter presumably a commission from the Würzburg bishop to Wibald von Stablo in Freising. If the document forgery battle ends in a deadlock because both parties have equally good creative scriptoria, then the one wins who has the troops and clears out the other's archive. [Anwander p. 692]

One is inclined to assume that the Reichenau archives were also cleared out in this way, as their archives were indeed destroyed; however, it is not known when this happened.

Arno Borst trivialises the motives of the time:
> Because Reichenau did not possess the instruments of precise confirmation deeds and comprehensive inventories of goods created in reform monasteries, the island monastery had to procure the legal basis at the beginning of the twelfth century by forging documents, not only for Reichenau itself, but also for other monasteries that were similarly endangered, Buchau, Lindau, Stein, Rheinau, Einsiedeln. [Borst p.175]

For some reason Reichenau had no deeds of ownership and, according to Borst, had to (!) 'procure' such rights and deeds. Borst, with his maudlin bias, does not see this correctly: you cannot create a right and a legal basis through forgeries!

The tactic of Reichenau in its constant struggle against the bishop was always to become imperially independent, i.e. it only wanted to be subject to the emperor and his law.

> Reichenau Monastery also attempted to free itself from the consecrating power and jurisdiction of the Bishop of Constance; Reichenau wanted to submit directly to the Pope in the manner of Cluny. [Borst p.175]

The abbey fought on several fronts: it wanted to submit to the emperor, but without losing property and rights to him. It also put out feelers to the Pope but quickly recognised the danger that the Pope could assign the abbey to the diocese. Reichenau was in a difficult situation, in a war with several fronts. The main front was not to be incorporated into the diocese of Constance.

There are four documents from this period for the village of Göggingen:
- The Richbold charter from the year 760
- The Bailiff's charter from 811
- The Walafried charter from 843
- and the Diethelm charter from 1202

The Richbold Charter
I, Richbold, hand over to the holy church, which was built in honour of St. Leodegar in the land of Alsace where Baldobert presides, and I want that the house itself become property, as well as in Alemannia, in the village called Cachinga, which lies above the Danube, ['in villa que dicitur Cachinga sitas super Danubium fluvium'] as well as in the place called Zozihuhus and in Chresinga, the property that I had in the very places

that I gave for the soul of my german brother Welponi, that is: all meadows, huts and manor houses, with waters, streams, money, animals, movable and immovable property. ... Murbach the 8th of August, in the year 9 under our lord Pipinus the King.

For a long time, the village of Göggingen was identified with the place name 'Cachinga'. But the Mainau lectures from 1952 already make it plausible that this cannot mean Göggingen:

> The name of the deserted village of Zuzelhausen in the Gächingen district of Münsingen fits much better, as there is a double z. One could even assume that it is a prescription for the correct "Zuziluhus". However, this also makes it clear that Cachinga refers to neighbouring Gächingen. The phonetic development of Cachinga to Gächingen is more conceivable than that of Cachinga to Göggingen, Stockach district, which has been claimed for this name up to now. In addition, neither Göggingen nor Gächingen is located on the Danube, where no corresponding place name can be found. On the other hand, Gächingen is situated on top of the Alb, i.e. in this sense "super Danubium fluvium", while Göggingen, seen from the Danube, can hardly be described as being situated above it. For all these reasons, the interpretation of the three place names as Gächingen, the former Zuzelhausen near Gächingen and Griesingen can be regarded as justified. [Basic questions of Alemannic history. Mainau lectures 1952. p. 118. Jan Thorbecke Verlag]

The Richbold charter thus defines the ownership claims of the monastery of Murbach in Alsace, which was a daughter monastery of Reichenau. Richbold is an invented count from Breisgau, and the only puzzling thing about the document is still the geographical indication 'sitas super danubium fluvium'

- situated on the upper Danube, or: situated above the Danube. Neither Gächingen nor Göggingen lie on the Danube. Admittedly, Göggingen is only 8 kilometres away from it. The document appears to be very old, probably dating back to the 11th century.

The word Cachinga in this document is highly unlikely to mean Göggingen.

The Bailiff's Charter

The following text gives us an impression of this document. It is not a full literal translation but gives the essentials in today's language:

Worms, 811 April 6.

In the holy name of the Trinity. Karl, by the divine favour of grace, Emperor Augustus. Since the Lord has made us princes and defenders of the churches, we must serve him so that we do not appear ungrateful, we must increase and defend the churches ...

Therefore, let it be known to all the faithful how the venerable Hatto, the abbot of the monastery called Sintleszesowa, went to the emperor and sadly complained: namely, most of the bailiffs who were supposed to represent the rights of the Church abused this right, so that those who should have been defenders shamelessly became rapacious and harmful executors ...

Therefore, whenever these bailiffs violate their duties, whether with property or with people, they shall immediately, and without further trial, lose their bailiwick ...

The bailiff shall keep the third part of his income for himself and pay two thirds to the abbot, and he may not appoint another bailiff without the abbot's permission.

No bailiff shall be allowed to administer justice on the island without the abbot's request....

For this purpose, we have designated three places outside the island where we grant the bailiff an annual assembly: Geggingen, Ermatingen and Wollmatingen. Each of these three places shall be given five bags of bread per year.

The bailiff may not speak against the will of the abbot in any way, may not force any servant of the House of God to a trial without the abbot's consent or approval, may not punish or control anyone from the familia without his just deliberation.

However, should there be a bailiff who violates this commandment, then he shall be deprived of the office without hope of recovery.

And so that this can be more firmly believed and more carefully observed, we have confirmed it below in our own hand and added it to our signet ring with an imprint.

The sign of Karl the High-born Emperor (Charlemagne) at 6 Idus Aprilis in the year of the Incarnation of the Lord DCCCXI.

This document has long since been recognised as a forgery. The "Württembergische Urkundenbuch online" provides the following explanation:

> The text impression follows the genuine confirmation of privileges issued by Emperor Heinrich VII in castris ante Florenciam, 1312 Oct. 17, into which the alleged original is inserted. The document is a forgery by the Reichenau Custos and Scholasticus Odalrich from the first half of the 12th century. [Jänichen: Reichenauer Fälscher, p. 279 ff; Hägermann: Urkundenfälschungen, p. 437 (on forgeries of charters on Charlemagne)]

The "Gesellschaft für ältere deutsche Geschichtskunde" (society for older german history) also takes the same view:

> Forgery without a genuine model from the first half of the 12th century, using a no longer extant document, perhaps the document of Karl III. from the last months of the year 887 for the protocol, the document of Heinrich

IV of 1065 for the Arenga and the chronicle of Hermann the Lame, for the personal names interspersed in the narrative text, produced by the same man who, through a series of forgeries, sought to raise the constitutional and canonical status of the abbey Reichenau again and also put his forgery skills at the service of other Swabian monasteries... Evidence from Lechner and Brandi, who, however, attributed these forgeries to the somewhat later Custos Odalrich. [Die Urkunden der Karolinger first volume 1906]

Karl Brandi writes:
In response to repeated complaints about the unjust claims and arrogance of the bailiffs, Charlemagne established their rights as follows: 1. the monastery bailiffs should be freely elected by the abbot and monks. No one shall claim a bailiwick under any legal title, especially not under the law of succession. 2. in the event of overstepping their authority or misconduct in office, the bailiffs shall lose their office without judgement...
- This text is freely composed. [Brandi1 p.44] This Reichenau document was the model for several other monasteries such as Buchau, Ottobeuren, Kempten, Lindau, Stein and Rheinau [Brandi1 p.107]
and he draws the conclusion: "It is a forgery by content and form, as by the connection with charters no. 8 and 35 obvious". [Brandi I p.14]

In the Acta Karolinorum, vol. 2, p. 435, Theodor Sickel writes:
A document of Karl [the Fat?] served as a model for the formulae and likewise such a document served as a model for the former document. This was seen by Bruschius in Reichenau, later it came to Ulm and from there to the Stuttgart archives. The document has been

published countless times, but its inauthenticity has been proven just as often.

The Landesarchivdirektion Baden-Württemberg (director of Baden-Württemberg archive) has come to the conclusion:

> This privilege is a forgery from the early 12th century, the text of which was put together from components of various older documents without a genuine template. The Reichenau monk responsible for this, who is not known by name, had demonstrably also put his forgery skills at the service of other Swabian monasteries at the time...
>
> In Heinrich VII's confirmation of privileges [1312], the inscribed document texts are externally separated from each other by the traced ruler's monogram and the signum lines reproduced in enlarged font. Reichenau Abbey was now interested to use the imperial confirmation to provide prominent proof of the authenticity of the documents presented and thus of its lordly status.

And Gustav Kempf writes in his Gögginger Dorfbuch: "This mention of our village as a bailiwick of Reichenau shows its importance for the early days of the monastery. The findings of this Carolingian forgery were then confirmed in a genuine document issued to the monastery by Emperor Heinrich VII on 23 October 1312 when he was in camp outside Florence on his roman campaign.

Arno Borst mentions the forgeries in a rather embarrassed manner, half excusing them and relativising them in an imaginative way:

> ... In Reichenau, more or less bona fide assumptions led to document forgeries as early as the tenth century, to the manipulation of a history as it should have been.

Bern and Hermann also had to delve into documents from the Carolingian and Ottonian periods, but both did so hesitantly, only when the legal situation was clear and even then without dogmatism. Because legal dispute was not really the monks' thing. Rather, both began to reflect on the historical conditions and limitations of monastic life. In doing so, they opened up a new, scientific dimension to monasticism, which simultaneously intensified and relativised the monks' mission. [Borst p.110]

But forgeries made out of good faith, with honest intentions, were certainly not the motive of the forger's workshop.

The fact that this bailiff's charter from the year 811 is not genuine therefore does not need to be explained in detail in future.
What is much more interesting is why it was produced, when it was produced and what its intention was.

The manuscript of this document is dated 1312 and is kept in the Stuttgart archives. The document, as it lies there today, is said to have been presented to Emperor Heinrich for confirmation in 1312 when he was on a military campaign in Florence. The core content of this document is the so-called insert, i.e. an alleged copy of a document from the year 811. The insert was not pasted in but the handwriting is the same throughout, the document was written in one piece. This raises questions: did an original copy of this insert ever exist? And was this document really presented to the emperor for confirmation in 1312?
In terms of content, it is a restriction of the imperial rights of the emperor's bailiffs, and why would the emperor seal something like this in his army camp outside Florence, of all places, where he certainly had other problems than confirming

such an ancient document, which was already 500 years old at the time (1312-811), and against his own imperial interests.

In 811, there was no dispute over bailiwick rights, which is the reason why the insert cannot date from that year. And in the 14th century, the bailiwick issue quickly lost its earlier significance. It can be assumed that the entire document, including the insert, was conceived and drawn up in the 14th century and that Emperor Heinrich never saw it.

It was surely made after 1313, when Emperor Heinrich was already dead. A dead emperor can no longer uncover a forgery bearing his name. The forger also chose the circumstances carefully: in the general chaos of the war, the emperor had certainly not taken his chancellery and his notaries with him to the army camp in Florence, so that the forgery could not be uncovered from this side either.

Here, in the midst of the war, the emperor alone allegedly executed the confirmation and affixed his seal, and his chancellery, which surely had remained at home, knew nothing about it. It was therefore pointless to question the imperial notaries about the authenticity of the document, as they had not been present. It was therefore almost impossible to uncover the forgery. And imperial wax seals can be forged.

In the early 14th century, someone had an interest in dividing the empire and Reichenau Abbey, separating them from each other. The abbey's quest for imperial immediacy was to be brought to an end. The emperor's protection was to be withdrawn.

The bailiff's charter is a masterpiece, not artistically but intellectually in terms of intrigue and masquerade. On the surface, it intends to benefit the abbey, but in fact has the exact opposite effect. If the Bishop of Constance is considered incapable of such a masterpiece, then there is only one possible forger and beneficiary: Venice. The bishop must have brought Venice and its master diplomats on board at the time; both had a common interest, namely to harm Reichenau.

The handwriting on the bailiff's deed clearly reads 'Geggingen'.
However, if you look at Gallus Öheim's chronicle from the 16th century, where this bailiff's deed was translated into german, then surprisingly we read "tettingen" rather than Geggingen[28].

For the annual meeting with the bailiff "outside the island", the bailiff's charter specifies the places Geggingen, Ermatingen and Wollmatingen.
However, Göggingen is quite far away from the other villages of Ermatingen and Wollmatingen, which are both close to Reichenau. Tettingen refers to the present-day village of Dettingen, which in turn is close to Reichenau, Wollmatingen and Ermatingen.
Logic tells us that the bailiff's deed did not actually refer to Göggingen at all, but to Dettingen. No one had realised this until now.

I wrote to the State Archives in Stuttgart about this, and they confirmed my suspicions when they replied: "As you have already been able to determine by comparing with Gallus Öheim, however, this does not match the two other places mentioned in the immediate vicinity of Reichenau. Tettingen (=Dettingen) is therefore the correct identification. Your suggestion makes it necessary to correct the misleading reference to Göggingen in the Württemberg Urkundenbuch".
See in the appendix.

---

28 see also here:
https://www.dmgh.de/mgh_dd_karol_i/index.htm#page/419/mode/
1up

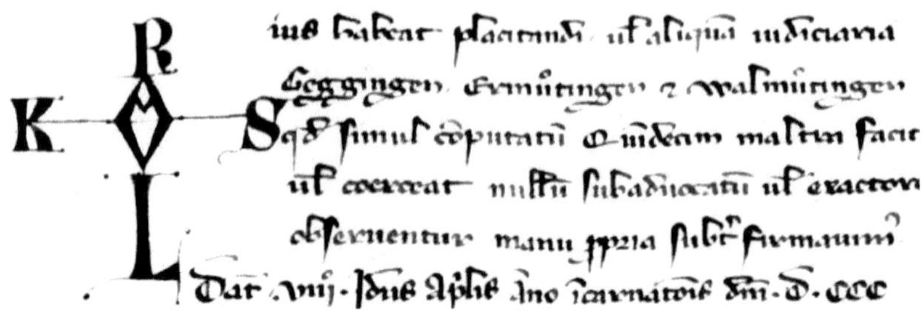

Fig. above: The bailiff's charter reads: "Geggingen, Ermutingen and Walmutingen"

Fig. above: Here in the Öheimchronicle one reads: "This is Tettingen, Hermandingen and Wolmatingen. Or whether it is the abbot's and bailiff's duty to almensdorff. On which these...".

It is not easy to explain why Geggingen is written once and Tettingen once. But it is highly probable that although the bailiff's deed undoubtedly states Geggingen, it actually refers to Dettingen. It is therefore probably impossible to draw conclusions from this bailiff's charter that Göggingen had a past as a Reichenau villication.

The bailiff's charter is properly written so that the forger's intention can be recognised and the forgery should be believed. This is not the case with the Walafried charter described below.

Festive procession in Reichenau-Mittelzell

Church St Georg in Reichenau-Oberzell,
built around 970.
(Painting by Vinzenz Marschall 1889-1959)

The Walafried Charter

It looks like a tax list for the cellar master of the monastery, strangely enough in the form of a sealed abbot's document. To get an impression, we have to read it in modern language. The translation was chosen quite freely for fluency, and the translation may not be entirely accurate in some cases. But that is irrelevant. Because anyone who delves too deeply into the details, as many historians do, will not see the wood for the trees. But you should have this overview in order to be able to assess this document.

The text:

In the name of the Holy Trinity. Walfred, Abbot of Augia, favoured by God, but unworthy ("quamvis indignus"). Let us determine what benefits and what kind of levies are to be given to our community in the storehouse each year. From Chuningesbach 10 reels of flax; likewise from Otelingen: In Marchelingen there must be 6 'mansari', which they must prepare. From Pirningen 10 bushels of vegetables, 100 cheese, a sheep, 4 baskets of yarn, 5 hemp, a barrel of honey. Likewise from Emphingen. The same applies to Pinestorf. From Meringen as well as from Wingen, and 12 jugs for the Nativity of the Lord and 50 goblets, and on the feast of St Michael also 12 jugs and 50 goblets, and likewise at Easter. From Tuttlingen as well as from Emphingen. All are to provide two fishing boats, one larger and one smaller. From Rodelingen and Honistetten ten bushels of flax, 100 barrels of cheese, a cauldron of honey, 50 measures of salt, 12 cauldrons of lard. From Easter to the feast of St Michael, the cellar master is given 6 pounds of bacon every week and 20 loaves of bread and enough leeks for the 'warmosium' every day.

Four cows must be given to the cellar master, one from Tuselingen, the second from Altheim, the third from Mülheim and the fourth from Thettingen, to be milked for the needy.

And these cows shall be housed in the brothers' garden and well looked after by the cellar master. But if one of these cows should die, the other must be replaced from the same town as the deceased cow. And 'warmosium' shall be given to the brothers every day, except on the days when they are fully on duty: and therefore, if one of the brothers does not eat from the three dishes given to them every day because of weakness of stomach, then at least the fourth dish, namely warmosium, should be served to him because of the mildness of this food...

From Steckborn 40 vine-growers must plant leeks in the garden of the brothers, each in 12 lines, and the servants of the wine waiter must cultivate and plant 12 fields; of the bearer they must plant 6 fields, of the host 6 fields. From Unlingen 100 cheeses, 10 bushels of vegetables, 1 cauldron of honey, 1 sheep and 5 bushels of flax.

Likewise from Altheim. Also from Gecgingen. Likewise from Münerdorf. From the east, they must hand over two fishing boats, one larger and one smaller, and they must build 4 houses for fishermen. From Langobardia 12 bushels of chestnuts, 5 barrels of oil, 40 beehives, 300 pounds of cheese...

From Almannsdorf 12 reels and a fishing boat. From Wolmatingen 10 reels. From Tettingen 10 reels. From Wolmatingen and Tettingen a larger fishing boat; and in Wolmatingen they have to prepare the husks and 34 measures of malt to prepare the husks. From Almannsdorf 17 rods for small-scale fishing in 'Lohen' ...

And in the upper lake the fishermen shall begin early in the morning to bring in the fish for a month and to eat a meal from the storehouse. And each fisherman should be given a glass of wine drawn by the brothers, with the bread, if he is old enough to be given it; but if he is young, let him accept the beer gratefully. The cellarer shall give a stick for catching fish, and two fishermen shall put it into the water, and two shall drive the fish through the Rhine channel, and the cellarer shall give each of them a glass of wine. And when the cellarer's messenger would come and order them to go, they should be ready at once, and no one should sit in that place of Lohen except four men who were fishermen. And every time, from Easter to 'Hagene', in the marshes and in these reedy places, four fishermen are commanded to fish, to have them ready with boats and other fishing gear, and after fishing to go into the cellar and have a meal, and from the birth of Christ the Lord to Easter every Sunday they are to come into the storeroom with their fish.

All these things that have been said above, we have decided with our elders that they must be given to the cellarer every year so that the brothers can quickly recover completely.

I, Sneuuart, a monk and deacon, wrote and sealed this letter from Abbot Walafred.

This was written on Augia on the calends of September, at the birth of the virgin Saint Verene and in the year of the incarnation of the Lord 843". -

A colourful jumble: 100 cheeses, flax, honey, cows, fishing boats, jugs, goblets, chestnuts from Italy and barrels full of oil, 6 pounds of bacon every week, 20 loaves of bread a day and enough leeks for the 'warmosium', some from this place too, and yes, from this village also, and from that place twice as much.

True to the motto: Would you like a little more?

Anyone with a practical mind immediately realises that this tax system is not realistic, that there is something wrong with it. Historians, on the other hand, have regarded this document as genuine for many centuries because they have obviously immersed themselves too much in the details and, as scholars, lacked practical imagination.

The formula in the year of the incarnation of the Lord 843 ("anno autem dominice incarnationis DCCCXLIII") alone makes it obvious that the text could not have been written in 843, as the dating "after the birth of Christ" only appeared after around the year 1000.

Karl Brandi notes the many scribal errors in the text and that a forger could not have invented all the levies for so many places due to a lack of documentary space, and then says:
> in the second half of the text there is only talk at all of the fishermen's levies. One must be clear about this in order not to get at a completely false picture of this monastic household: the point of the forgery is directed against the monastery's fishing community. [Brandi I p.44]

The regulations for the fishermen, however, are so confused and impractical that one can suspect more behind them than a mere jab at the fishermen's co-operative. Who in their right mind would instruct their tax-paying fishermen how to catch their fish? Two fishermen should scare up the fish, two should drive them into the net... As if the fishermen themselves didn't know best how to catch fish.

> The outer form of the document is also unusual:
> The alleged document of Abbot Walahfrid is written on two pieces of parchment, roughly stapled together and very poorly worked; the front and back of both are equally rough. The lower piece bears a genuine Arnolf seal properly attached; its inscription seems to have been deliberately blurred and made indistinct by a wax after-casting, as the raised head stands out much more sharply. -
> The forms of the imperial charters are imitated by the elongated script in the usual lines and in an almost monstrous sign of recognition. The letters of the elongated script are partly formed quite arbitrarily; one

notices how the forger, in the absence of any pattern, confines himself here to giving the large letters familiar to him the most grandiose form possible. ... Correspondingly, the line spacing is small and disorganised. [Brandi I p.55]

Fig.: Text sample of the Walafried document from 1 September 843: "elongated script, monstrous names, letters with a grandiose shape".

This is how Hansmartin Schwarzmaier also sees it:
> ... The script is elongated in the first line, the intitulatio and invocatio are taken from the form of the royal charter. This part is particularly bizarre and clumsy, an ugly product of antiquated letter forms in a chaotic style. [Schwarzmaier p. 25]

It was not until 1888 that the Walafried document was exposed as a forgery by archivist Aloys Schulte[29]:
> It is well known that the archives of Reichenau were not under a good star, because even in the 15th century Gallus Öheim did not know many more documents from the monastery's flowering period that we still have today. The neighbouring Abbey of St. Gallen, which is usually mentioned in the same breath as Reichenau because of its related fates, has left us an extremely rich source in numerous documents on donations and exchange

---

29 in: Zeitschrift für die Geschichte des Oberrheins vol 3 Neue
     Folge 42 (1888)

agreements, from which we can establish the history of the monastery and its extensive possessions and thus also of large areas of Switzerland and Swabia. This treasure trove of documents takes us back to the time of the monastery's flowering period and supplements the reports of the historians that the monastery produced. Reichenau is different. All that has survived from the flowering period of this monastic island before the year 1100 are a few imperial and royal charters, the majority of which have long been recognised as forgeries ...

In the document, the exact wording of which follows the original in the enclosure, 'Walfredus deo favente Augiensium abbas', together with the monastery elders, supposedly decrees what income and burdens are to be given to the common cellar in consideration of the present and future welfare of the brothers. It lists, place by place, the beans, vegetables, leeks, chestnuts, oil, cheese, sheep, honey, lard, bacon, bread, cows, salt, as well as kettles, bowls and pots for the use of the kitchen, but first and foremost hemp, hair ropes, fishing boats, brushwood and fishing nets for the fishing carried out by the monastery. Finally, the obligations of the fishermen are set out in detail.

Anyone who reads the text of the document with some attention will be puzzled to discover word forms such as Marchelungen, Emphingen, Tuselingen, Meringen, Tuttelingen, Gecgingen etc., which do not fit the 9th century at all. In real documents Meringen 882 is called: Mereheninga, Tuselingen 802: Tusilinga, Tuttlingen 803: Tuttilininga; how is the abbreviated ending 'ingen' conceivable in the 9th century? ...

The third argument alone, however, should have been enough to cast suspicion on the document; it is the artless, barbaric language that the forger puts into Walafried's mouth. ...

The document is not written on one sheet of parchment, but on two, with the seal imprinted on the lower one. The two sheets are attached by a strip of parchment drawn through both. It would therefore be easy to separate the two sheets from each other and to reattach another sheet instead of the first. The content and authenticity of the upper part of the document is therefore not in the least guaranteed by the seal. ...

The script of the context of the document does not even attempt to imitate the Carolingian script.

After what has been said, there is no longer any question that this document also belongs to the large number of Reichenau forgeries already known [Schulte].

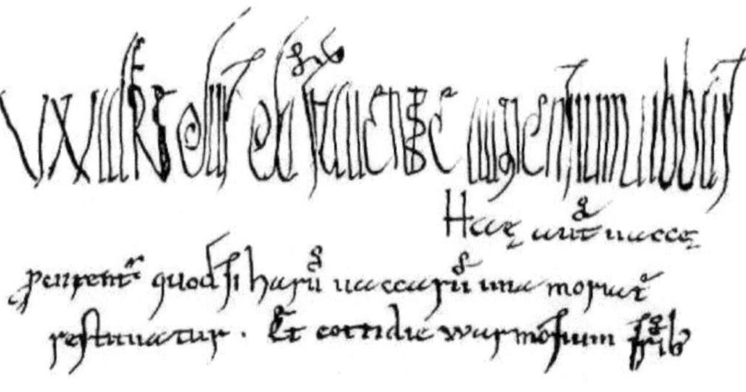

Fig.: Excerpts from the document of 1 Sept. 843. "Letters extraordinarily coarse" [Brandi].
First line: Walfredus deo favente augensium abbas - Walafried of God's favour abbot of Reichenau
[Brandi I, table 11]

If you read the text of the document carefully, then the listed taxes seem to be only a small part of the total taxes paid to the monastery. Not all the villages liable to pay taxes are listed. Wine as a taxable good is missing entirely.
If you read carefully, the levies listed must have been given to

the monastery for the purpose of caring for the sick monks. To this end, the villages had to grow leeks, give cows for milk, catch fish, deliver bread and bacon and olive oil from Italy.
There is talk of 'warmosium' to be given to the sick friars, which is warm milk with leeks to make the friars well in the event of an upset stomach.

So who produced such a bad forgery in the middle of the 12th century, and why? It was clear to anyone who read it that something could not be right here. The outer form, the monstrous letters and, above all, the content.
"My village is supposed to pay so much tax because of a few sick brothers?" Catching small fish in the muddy reeds at dawn every day from Easter to "Hagene"? Deliver a cow every year and build fishing boats? Deliver barrels of honey and bring sheep to the island, along with hemp. The list of taxes is so unbelievably arbitrary that you think the writer has let his imagination run wild - 100 cheeses, no let's make it 300, 10 reels of flax? Better 12. 34 bushels of malt, 17 fishing rods. Pure fantasy figures. "Would you like a little more?"

This Walafried charter was certainly not fabricated to generate income for the monastery. This would not have required a document in the form of a royal charter with a seal. The purpose was probably quite clearly to turn the villages against the monastery, to divide the monastery with the villages. This deed did not benefit the monastery, but harmed it and was directed against it.
If this is the case, and there is every indication that it is, then this document must be regarded as a masterpiece. The usual suspect is Venice, which also forged Byzantine coins on a grand scale, not to enrich itself but to weaken its competitor Constantinople with counterfeit money.
While the bailiff's deed was intended to give the appearance of authenticity, the Walafried charter was intended to look fake

from the beginning. Even a farmer who could not read the contents would become suspicious when he saw the outer form of the document. And that was the purpose.

A royal charter indeed, with a seal and grandiose letters, but of a sloppy nature and suspiciously confused content. Impressive and awe-inspiring on the one hand, but highly suspicious on the other - what village mayor would not have been confused after being presented with this document?

As Brandi assumes, the Walafried document probably dates from around 1150, at the latest from 1165, it was probably drawn up by the monastery administrator and archivist Odalrich, and the village of Göggingen is mentioned in it as "gecgingen".

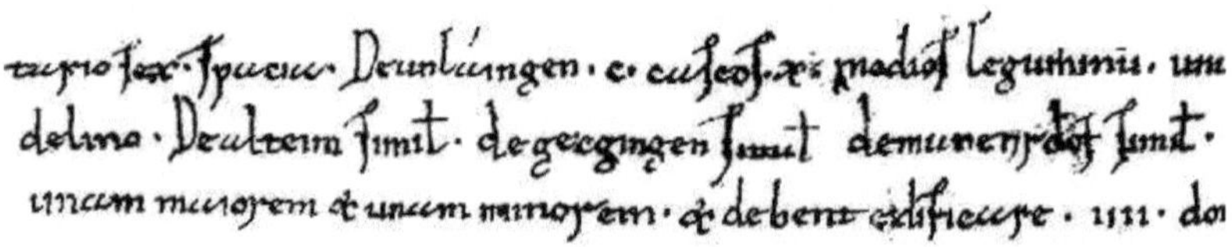

Enlargement:

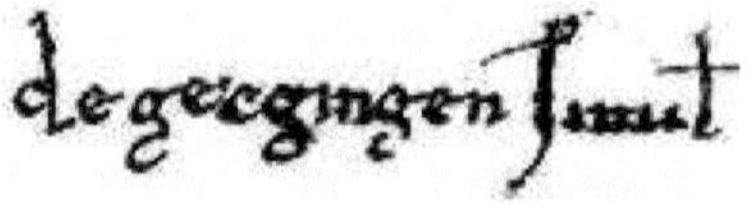

Centre line: De alteim similiter. de gecgingen similiter de munersdorf similiter ("similar also from Altheim. Also from gecgingen. Also from Mindersdorf"). - From the Walafried deed.

One has to wonder how Odalrich managed to erase all the old royal charters that were valuable to the monastery and replace them with new texts. Did nobody notice? Was it done in agreement with the abbot? That is unthinkable. The abbot was always in favour of his monastery, while Odalrich's forgery workshop was clearly on the opposite side. Odalrich was an agent of the other side and was not on the side of Reichenau Abbey. Odalrich probably did not fabricate his documents on Reichenau, but had them written abroad. This was the only way he could avoid arousing the suspicions of the abbot and the convent. It was probably also Odalrich who cleared out the entire document archive at the instigation of Venice.

None of the other monasteries in the area had such serious problems as Reichenau. But all other monasteries did not have St Mark as their patron saint and did not have Venice as their opponent.

Arno Borst sees a coalition of embittered abbeys that were driven to forgery out of pure bitterness, and also mentions that other monasteries had long since achieved what Reichenau had always striven for: freedom of the monastery from the emperor and bishop.

> Because Reichenau did not possess the instruments of precise confirmation deeds and comprehensive inventories of goods that were created in reform monasteries, the island monastery had to procure the legal basis at the beginning of the twelfth century by forging documents, not only for Reichenau itself, but also for other monasteries that were similarly jeopardised, Buchau, Lindau, Stein, Rheinau and Einsiedeln.
>
> A new kind of solidarity in the Lake Constance region, a coalition of the embittered. It fought in the dark for achievements that reform monasteries such as Schaffhausen had long enjoyed: free election of the abbot by the convent, restriction of obligations to the king, definition of the powers of the monastery bailiff,

overall liberation of the monastery from external influences and strengthening of its internal self-discovery. [Borst p.175]

The immense moral abuses and distortions, fires, feuds, insolence of the monastery lords and devastation that Reichenau experienced were not seen in Buchau, Lindau, Stein etc. and certainly not in the reform monasteries. It didn't happen anywhere else.
Only Reichenau had St Mark as a relic...
In this respect, we must also relieve Abbot Eberhard Brandis, who allegedly burnt all the old fief books before 1350, only to create new fief books immediately afterwards. No abbot works against his own monastery. It is reasonable to assume that Brandis found an empty archive when he took office.

The Diethelm Charter
The Diethelm charter, from which many villages, including Göggingen, derive their possible first historical mention, probably did not originate from the Reichenau forgery workshop of the 12th century.
The translated latin text reads as follows (translation mistakes are possible, but not relevant for understanding):

"Diethelmus, by the grace of God Bishop of the Church of Constance and Abbot of the Church of Augens [Reichenau]. Let it be generally known that we and the church of Augens have embraced the church of Salem until now with a special privilege of love, trusting in the Lord that we serve God there and here and in the future by merits and prayers and will always be supported by God, that the venerable Eberhardus, abbot of Salem, and his brothers, were redeemed by Beringer, a soldier of town Messkirch[30], the fief which he had in

---

30 'Beringero milite de Meschilchi'

Hohinberc from Count Mangold of Rordorf and seized it from our hands by giving him 70 pounds. But afterwards the count exchanged the said fee with the said Beringer with our church of Augens, on condition that the said fee should be transferred to the church of Salem. And the above Mangold, as compensation for the sum of money, gave our church a property he had in Thisindorf and another in a place called Waltfurt, together with some men in Messkirch.

And we have, with the consent of the brothers and pastors of our church of Augens, transferred the special property in Hohinberc to the church of Salem as a perpetual possession. But in order that this agreement might continue, two servants of the church of Augens, namely Bertoldus the administrator of **Gegingen** and Albertus de Crauchenwis, together with five other servants of the church, swore that the compensation was paid by the above mentioned. The payment to our church is more favourable to the aforementioned estate in Hohinberc. These events took place in our above-mentioned village of Gegingen. In the year of the incarnation of the Lord 1202, and the witnesses are: The aforementioned Count Mangold of Rordorf. Heinrich of Fridingin. Wernherus Galli. Bertholdus the administrator of **Gegingen** and his son Berthold. Albertus de Cruchinwis. Heinrich de Crauchenwis and his brother Eberhard. Heinrich of Abilach. Conradus, minister of Augia. Liutfridus de Rordorf and Cunradus, who bears the surname 'Child'. Berthold and Wernherus de Menningen and many others".

Fig.: Bertoldus videlicet villicus de gegingen (from Diethelm charter)

It is important to know that Diethelm of Krenkingen first became Abbot of Reichenau in 1169 and was later (1189) also appointed Bishop of Constance by the Hohenstaufen dynasty. In the last years of his life, he was almost never on site, but almost always travelling on political missions for the empire. Shortly before his death in 1206, he resigned the abbacy of Reichenau and spent his last months as a simple monk in Salem Monastery near Lake Constance. It is said that he was a great friend and patron of Salem.

This Diethelm document has special features:
- It is incompletely dated
- It is a retroactive confirmation
- It is a complicated real estate triangular transaction
- A soldier plays an important role
- Witnesses are named who cannot testify to the original exchange transaction, but only retroactively testify to what the Diethelm deed specifies. They can therefore only testify to the written text, but not to the transaction itself.
- The exchange transaction is to the disadvantage of Reichenau

The 'Zeitschrift für die Geschichte des Oberrheins' 1876 writes:
> ... Also on 7 June 1202 Diethelm of Krenkingen is in Constance, acting as arbitrator in a matter concerning the churches of Mauchen and Betmaringen. But he also issued a document for the covetous Salem monastery in Göggingen near Messkirch, unfortunately without a date, in which he expresses his very special preference for that place of worship and leaves a fiefdom to Homberg as his own. Once again, however, it was his Reichenau monastery, not the diocese of Constance, from whose funds he was generous. But while the pious brothers of Salem made one acquisition after another,

they complained about their bitter poverty.

For the following reasons, this Diethelm document should be regarded as false and a later invention:
It is very unusual for a document to contain only a year but no day. But the forger does not know what his alleged witnesses were doing on a specific day; perhaps some of them were demonstrably absent, on a military campaign, on a visit or travelling somewhere else. To ensure that no-one can discover his forgery in this way, he omits the exact date.
The barter transaction is merely a retroactive confirmation of a (seemingly) genuine exchange that took place a long time before. The actual contracting parties are not even present. Of course, this makes it easy to claim or agree something in a sham contract.
This business 'over many corners' makes it difficult to prove a counterfeit. The Abbot of Salem gives a man named Beringer, who had an estate from Count Mangold, 70 pounds in money. But then Mangold and Beringer exchanged the 70 pounds with Reichenau on the condition that the fee was to be transferred to the church of Salem. And as compensation for this sum of money, Mangold gave Salem a property he had in Thisindorf and another in a place called Waltfurt.
None of this makes any sense and it smells of fraud.
A soldier named Beringer from Meßkirch receives the money for a farm that Mangold supposedly owns. Mangold in turn gives the money to Reichenau and tells them to give it to Salem. And then Mangold gives the Salem monastery property from Reichenau as compensation for the money. Soldier Beringer from Messkirch, who presumably never existed, is given the role of a straw man.

Incidentally, this Diethelm document could be one of the earliest mentions of Messkirch, as Messkirch was certainly built for the first time not before 1120, when medival towns were founded. You can see the plan of the town in its layout, where the chalice ("kelch") that gives the town its name can still be seen today. However, the original name of the town was soon forgotten and confused, as the church was then called 'Kilche' in german, as it is still pronounced in Switzerland today (Swiss German 'kille, killa' = german 'Kirche' = church). This is how the name changed from Mess-kelch to Mess-kirche. And Heimrad's vita, in which Messkirch is associated with the year 1080, is an invention.

The result of the Salem triangular deal was important for the forger to mention at the end, because who else would have had the overview:

> And we have, with the consent of the brothers and pastors of our church of Augens, transferred the special estate in Hohinberg to the church of Salem as a perpetual possession.

Perpetual possession is always good and important. We see the transfer of ownership from Reichenau to Salem, although Reichenau had nothing to do with the alleged original exchange. And unnamed priests and friars of Reichenau allegedly agreed to the deal. A scheme that can be seen repeatedly also in other charters.

It is therefore a classic barter transaction at the expense of third parties, in this case at the disadvantage of Reichenau.

The Diethelm deed must have been drawn up long after Diethelm's death (1206), when Reichenau was for some reason unable to defend itself. And who would doubt a deed of gift from their own former abbot in retrospect?

The Diethelm deed of the alleged year 1202 was probably not written in 1202, but many years later. Someone used this trick in the early 13th century to misappropriate the property of Reichenau, and not just with this one Diethelm deed from

1202. Quite obviously, several false documents were drawn up in the name of Diethelm of Krenkingen:

In the Codex salemitanus there are about a dozen documents from Diethelm without a date of notarisation. The pattern is always the same: opaque triangular transactions, retroactive confirmations, no real witnesses, disadvantage for Reichenau, advantage for Salem. And several other times the scam is played with soldiers allegedly involved, a soldier from the Höri or elsewhere, a soldier Bertold appears, a Rudolf soldier from Ramsberg, Ulrich soldier from Bodman, a soldier without a name, then several soldiers again, and so on.
Soldiers have the advantage that they are not locals, never live in the same place for long, but have to go to war from time to time and can perish there. The most important witness is then unfortunately unknown or missing. Who is then able to prove a forgery?

Are the Diethelmurkunde and its incompletely dated counterparts also a work of Venice? One can assume so because of the sophistication shown here.

See also, for example, Helmut Maurer: Das Bistum Konstanz 5: Die Konstanzer Bischöfe vom Ende des 6. Jahrhunderts bis 1206 (Germania Sacra N. F. 42,1):
> ... a direct enfeoffment of episcopal ministerials also emerges from an undated document of Bishop Diethelm for Salem Abbey. This document states that Berthold, known as "Soldier from Höri", together with his wife and children, had transferred an estate in Watt into the hands of Conrad of Castell, as they were both ministerials of the Church of Constance. Conrad of Castell was then to hand it over to the monks of Salem with the bishop's consent.

A possible anniversary of Göggingen could therefore refer to the deed of foundation of the Wald monastery[31] from 1212, even if there are also possible dating problems here, or better still to the Walafried charter, which was written in 1165 at the latest, with its interesting and illustrious background.

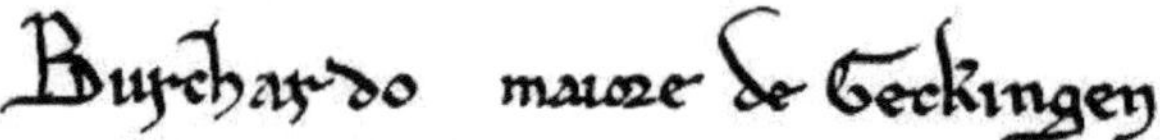

Fig.: Mention of the village of Göggingen in the foundation charter of the monastery of Wald in 1212: "Burchardo maior de Geckingen".

"The forgeries begin in New Testament times and have never ceased" [32]

---

31 see Freiburg Diocesan Archives Volume 12 1878
32 The protestant theologian Carl Schneider in: 'Geistesgeschichte der christlichen Antike', 1976.

Appendix

Dear Ladies and Gentlemen,

I am a local historian, come from Göggingen / Baden and am currently researching the Reichenau documents (forgeries) concerning the documents of my home village.

The 'Württembergische Urkundenbuch' edits the document of 6 April 811 (bailiffs deed, Charlemagne) as follows:

Tria, non alia loca extra insulam ad hoc deputavimus et determinavimus, in quibus eos rite annuatim placitum habere concessimus; scilicet apud Geggingen, Ermutingen et Walmutingen, vel si magis utrique, abbat ...

Gallus Öheim translates this passage as follows:

... this is Tettingen, Hermandingen and Wolmatingen, ...

I have attached the handwritten source from Öheim in the email: here you can clearly read: not geggingen but Tettingen. ("This is tettingen, hermandingen and wolmatingen").

Karl Brandi also writes from Öheim: 'tettingen'.

[Karl Brandi: History of Reichenau Abbey. The Chronicle of Gallus Öhem. 1893. page 45].

The Württemberg document book writes: Geggingen, but Gallus Öheim and Brandi, however, write: tettingen (=Dettingen).

Now, of course, it would be interesting for me to know whether my home village of Göggingen is actually mentioned in this document from 811, or whether Dettingen is meant.

Logically, Dettingen should be meant, because it is close to the two other villages Ermatingen and Wollmatingen, whereas Göggingen doesn't really fit here because of its distance from Reichenau.

Perhaps this document has already been digitised. Could you perhaps send me a scan of the part of the original document where I can see the word Geggingen / Tettingen itself, if possible in context with some other words or phrases.

Thank you very much.

With kind regards, Herbert Fiessinger

The State Archive in Stuttgart answered:

Dear Mr Fießinger,

You can use the entry in the Württemberg document book to determine all the relevant contexts of Charlemagne's alleged deed of 811 for Reichenau Abbey:

http://www.wubonline.de/?wub=134

The document is a forgery that was produced by Reichenau Abbey in the 12th century without a genuine original and was authenticated in 1312 by emperor Henry VII in 1312.

This authentication by Henry VII from 1312 is printed in the Württemberg document book, according to HStA Stuttgart H 51 U 229. This document is available in digital form:

http://www.landesarchiv-bw.de/plink/?f=1-1259888-1

It clearly reads Geggingen, as it is also reproduced in the WUB. However, as you have already been able to determine by comparing it with Gallus Öheim, this does not match the two other places mentioned in the immediate vicinity of Reichenau. Tettingen (=Dettingen) is therefore the correct identification, and this is also the place name given in the authoritative edition of the document of 811 in the MGH (MGH DDKarol. I. No. 281, p. 419 below):

https://www.dmgh.de/mgh_dd_karol_i/img/150/mgh_dd_karol_i_00428.jpg. Your comment makes it necessary to correct the misleading reference to Göggingen in the Württembergisches Urkundenbuch. With thanks and kind regards, Erwin Frauenknecht

---

Left: Spalatin (+1545). Centre: Cardinal Contarini (+1542). Right: The 75. Venetian Doge Leonardo Loredan (+1521, picture is from 1501)

The Walafried charter (upper half):

In the third last line: "gecgingen"

To the right of the Carolus monogram: "Geggingen"

Literature

Anwander Gerhard (2000): Von Klöstern, Karolingern und Konkordat. Zeitensprünge Dez. 2000, S. 680, Mantis Verlag
Badische Landesbibliothek, Cod. Aug. perg. 84, fol. 114r: Report on Cardinal Marco Barbo's visit to Reichenau in 1474; Cod. Aug. pap. 14, fol. 152v
Beyerle (Hrsg.) (1925): Die Kultur der Abtei Reichenau Band 1. Verlag der Münchner Drucke.
Bock Sebastian: Das Markusgrab im Münster von Reichenau-Mittelzell, Heidelberg:
arthistoricum.net, 2022 (Studien zur Kunst- und Kulturgeschichte am Oberrhein, Band 3).
Published on 20 Dec. 2022 - No page references, as only online.
https://books.ub.uni-heidelberg.de/arthistoricum/catalog/book/1138
Borst Arno: Mönche am Bodensee
Borst Arno: Hermann der Lahme. Hegau - Zeitschrift für Geschichte, Heft 32/33 1975/76
Brandi Karl (1890): Die Geschichte der Abtei Reichenau I: Die Reichenauer Urkundenfälschungen
Brandi Karl (1893): Die Geschichte der Abtei Reichenau II: Die Chronik des Gallus Öhem
Dennig Regina und Zettler Alfons (1996): Der Evangelist Markus in Venedig und in Reichenau, in Zeitschrift für die Geschichte des Oberrheins page 144
Farrell Joseph: Financial Vipers of Venice; Babylon's Banksters
Gröber Conrad (1922): Reichenauer Kunst
Gröber Conrad (1938): Die Reichenau
Güßfeldt E. (1894): Die Insel Reichenau und ihre Klostergeschichte
Hoffmann Volker: Der St. Galler Klosterplan - einmal anders gesehen, in: Zeitensprünge April 1995, Mantis Verlag

Illig Heribert (1996): Das erfundene Mittelalter

Illig Heribert (2017): Des Kaisers leeres Bücherbrett. Wer bewahrte das antike Erbe?

Kempf Gustav (1969): Das Gögginger Dorfbuch

Knittel Helmut: Walahfrid Strabo Visio Wettini, Thorbeke Verlag

Nobbe K. (1893): Die Chronik Herimanns von Reichenau

Reisser Emil (1960): Die frühe Baugeschichte des Münsters zu Reichenau

Richter Michael (1996): Neues zu den Anfängen des Klosters Reichenau, in Zeitschrift für die Geschichte des Oberrheins, vol. 144

Schwarzmaier Hansmartin: Die Gründungsurkunden der Reichenau

Schulte Aloys (1925) in: Die Kultur der Reichenau Band 1

Staiger Franz Xaver (1860): Die Insel Reichenau im Untersee

Untermann, Matthias (2001): Die archäologische Erforschung der Insel Reichenau; in: *Arbeitsheft 8 des Landesdenkmalamts Baden-Württemberg,* Stuttgart; pages 157-171

Vogturkunde (Bailiffs charter digital): http://www.landesarchiv-bw.de/plink/?f=1-1259888-1

Walafriedurkunde digital: http://www.landesarchiv-bw.de/plink/?f=4-3883698-1

Zettler Alfons: Die politischen Dimensionen des Markuskults im hochmittelalterlichen Venedig

On Venice, see also the books by Webster Tarpley